WILD LIFE THROUGH THE YEAR

Also by Richard Morse

THE OPEN BOOK OF WILD LIFE

With colour plates, photographs, drawings

" A book I should be glad to give to my
children ; it is also a book I should be
glad for my children to give to me."

H. E. BATES

★

Black's Nature Pocket Books

by E. H. B. Boulton
BRITISH TREES

by Charles A. Hall
BRITISH WILD FLOWERS
BRITISH BIRDS
BRITISH BUTTERFLIES & MOTHS
BRITISH BIRDS' EGGS & NESTS

by Richard Morse
WILD LIFE THROUGH THE YEAR

BOOK
PRODUCTION
WAR ECONOMY
STANDARD

Roland Green.

GOLDFINCHES.

WILD LIFE
THROUGH THE YEAR

by

RICHARD MORSE, F.L.S.

AUTHOR OF "THE OPEN BOOK OF WILD LIFE," ETC.

WITH SIXTEEN COLOUR PLATES
FORTY PHOTOGRAPHS AND MANY DRAWINGS

ADAM & CHARLES BLACK
4, 5 & 6 SOHO SQUARE LONDON W.1

PREFACE

In preparing this small guide to the wild life of the countryside, I have not attempted to describe the plants and animals themselves. That is the task of the other volumes in the series to which the present book belongs. I have tried, rather, to draw attention to their behaviour, and especially to that behaviour which is related to the changing seasons of the year.

The book is based largely upon my own observations and records over a number of years, and I hope very much that it will encourage many of its readers to keep similar Nature diaries of their own. I hope, too, that it will help them to discover, at first hand, something of that deep and lasting pleasure which comes from *observing* living things, without any thought of harming or destroying them.

It will be seen that there are two quite different ways in which a book of this kind can be used. If you wish, for example, to get a broad idea of what the birds are doing throughout the year, you can read the monthly sections on bird life *consecutively*. If, on the other hand, you wish to know something of the sights and sounds that await you in the fields on any particular day of the year, you can read the notes for the appropriate month *as a whole*.

Since the book deals with an inexhaustible subject, it is necessarily incomplete. I trust, however, that it will serve as a simple introduction to the hobby which inspired Gilbert White to write *The Natural History of Selborne*, and which has brought so much joy into the lives of so many others ever since.

RICHARD MORSE.

FIRST PUBLISHED 1942
MADE IN GREAT BRITAIN

CONTENTS

NOTE

IN reading this book it should be remembered that the dates assigned to the different events will vary considerably, not only in different regions in the same year, but also in the same region in different years. They must therefore be regarded as approximate only.

The separation of Bird Life from Animal Life in the notes, moreover, is merely for the reader's convenience, and must not be taken to suggest that the birds belong to a different kingdom.

The twelve whole-page line drawings, one for each month, have been done specially for this work by Miss Doris Meyer.

ILLUSTRATIONS

IN THE TEXT

CHAPTER I

JANUARY

INTRODUCTORY

IT is always a good plan to begin a study of Nature as early as possible in the new year. In January, wild life as a whole is at a low ebb. In June it is at flood-tide. In the first month of the year, therefore, you are far less likely to be overwhelmed by the sheer exuberance of living things. The actors on the stage are now relatively few, and you have a much better chance of becoming acquainted with them in the height of summer, when their numbers are almost bewilderingly great.

Another advantage of beginning your studies in January is that the early start enables you to appreciate far more fully the wonder and beauty of the supreme drama of life. You can follow it, month by month, up to its magnificent crescendo at midsummer, and then, again month by month, down to its nadir at the end of the year. It is a drama of inexhaustible variety, and you can watch it for a lifetime without ever growing weary.

Our calendar, it is true, speaks of January as the second month of winter, but the naturalist prefers to regard it as the first month of spring. One of the great joys of a study of Nature, indeed, is the joy of beginning your spring on the very first day of the new year. And you can, in fact, always do that, for January never comes without bringing unmistakable signs of the spring that is to follow.

PLATE I.

HIVE BEES IN WINTER.

They are clustering together in the interior of the hive.

Richard Morse, F.L.S.

THE WINTER HELIOTROPE.

The chapters of this little book are intended to introduce you, at the proper season, to a few of the players in Nature's great drama, and to a few of the parts that they play. But such introductions must not for one moment, of course, be regarded as a substitute for the drama itself. At most they can be nothing more than a very fragmentary guide to it. To appreciate the charm of the play to the full, you must see it for yourself, and you must watch it in the open air the whole year round.

BIRD LIFE IN JANUARY

One of the first of the spring singers to attract your attention in January is the song-thrush. Very often you can hear him singing with great vigour on New Year's Day, and if the weather is not too severe he will continue with scarcely a break throughout the month.

If you are a beginner in the study of bird song, you should listen very carefully to these early efforts of the song-thrush, because he is certain to be joined, sooner or later, by the mistle-thrush (PLATE 3), whose voice is very similar in character. The loud, wild song of this larger bird, however, is quite distinct, and with a little practice you can distinguish either bird in a moment.

Other regular singers of early January are the robin, the starling and the dipper ; and long before the end of the month you will hear the thin little song of the hedge-sparrow, and the ringing calls of the great tit (PLATE 3) and the blue tit. Linnets, wrens, skylarks and a number of other birds will also sing at intervals if the weather remains mild.

In the woods our three common species of woodpeckers can

B

all be heard calling in January, each in its own distinctive manner. The hard, shrill *Pee-pee-pee-pee-pee-pee* of the barred woodpecker is just as unmistakable as the more familiar *Plu-plu-plu-plu-plu-plu* of the green species, while the sudden *Chick* of the pied wood-pecker is utterly different from both.

It is not merely in their voices, however, that the birds are

FIG. 1.—TWO BRAMBLINGS.
The birds are seeking beech-mast in the snow.

showing signs of spring. In many cases their plumage is changing too. The black-headed gull, for instance, which has been an almost white-headed gull since the end of last summer, is already donning his familiar dark hood ; and the gradual wearing away of the cock-sparrow's breast feathers is now bringing to light the black cravat that will make him such a proud and distinguished person when the real spring draws near.

Associating with the chaffinches that search for beechnuts among the thick carpets of fallen leaves, even when these are sprinkled with snow, the brambling, or bramble-finch, may often be seen. He is a winter visitor to this country, and is sometimes mistaken for a chaffinch. You will know him in a moment, however, by the characteristic patch of white on the lower part of his back, which is very conspicuous as he flies away from you (FIG. I).

ANIMAL LIFE IN JANUARY

Our native mammals are not usually so ready as our birds to show early signs of spring in either their behaviour or their dress, but one of them, at least, is ready to remind you that a new year has begun.

Our foxes, as a rule, are peculiarly silent animals—much more so, for instance, than their near relations, the dogs and the wolves —but in January, which is the chief month of their mating season, the vixen screams and the dog-fox yelps in the early hours of the darkness, or even during the night.

The scream of the vixen is a strange, eerie sound, which has often been likened to the scream of a peacock, while the loud yelp of her mate is rather like the twice-uttered bark of a dog, repeated at short intervals.

But the January activities of most of our mammals will, of course, vary with the weather. Some of them—such as the dormice —are now hibernating, and even some of the more active ones— such as the voles—will lie low for a time if the weather is severe. When days and nights are mild, however, large numbers of them will be abroad, and their footprints in the soft earth will give written evidence of their wanderings (PLATE 3).

Most of our bats are still asleep, and large colonies of pipistrelles —our commonest species—can sometimes be found in old hollow trees, or under the roofs of churches and barns (PLATE 3). In a mild winter, however, it is not at all a rare event to see a pipistrelle on the wing, even in January.

Hive bees, too, are mostly dormant at this season (PLATE 1), though they also will come out when the weather is mild. The queen wasp, however, is a sounder sleeper, and is scarcely likely to awaken until March or April. You may see her to-day clinging tightly to an old curtain or window-frame (PLATE 3).

A typical moth of the month is the pale brindled beauty. The male insect often comes to the farmer's lantern after dusk, but the female is a wingless, spidery creature, and must be sought on tree trunks and fences (PLATE 3).

PLANT LIFE IN JANUARY

Although a good many of January's wild flowers are mere stragglers from last year—such as the ever-present groundsel (PLATE 3), for example—a few at least may be looked upon as real new-comers that are tough and hardy enough to brave the winter's

---

KEY TO PLATE 3

1. Mistle-thrush singing.
2. Pale brindled beauty moth, male and female.
3. Pipistrelle bat asleep.
4. Male flowers of yew.
5. Great tit calling.
6. Queen wasp hibernating on curtain.
7. Winter aconite.
8. Groundsel in flower and fruit.
9. Gorse in flower.
10. Yellow wall-lichen.
11. Footprints of water vole.
12. Rough-stalked feather-moss.

PLATE 3.

JANUARY

FROM A JANUARY SKETCHBOOK.
(*See opposite page.*)

cold. Prominent among these are the winter heliotrope (PLATE 2), the winter aconite (PLATE 3), the snowdrop and the dog's mercury.

It is true that the winter heliotrope and the winter aconite are not real natives of this country, but both have firmly established

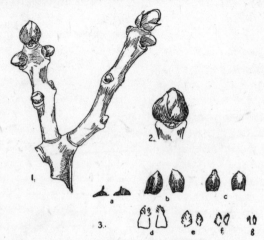

FIG. 2.—ASH TWIG IN JANUARY.

1. Twig with winter buds.   2. Bud enlarged.
3. Bud dissected, showing transition from scales to foliage leaves.
a, b, c. The first three pairs of scales.   *d, e, f.* Typical inner-scales.
g. First pair of foliage leaves.

themselves in many places. The winter heliotrope is deliciously fragrant, and if kept well within bounds is a very desirable tenant for a rough corner of the garden.

In mild Januaries the gorse (PLATE 3) and the yew (PLATE 3) often flower freely, but even if these and other blossoms are held back by cold weather, the buds of our bare trees are always available, and they are often no less interesting in structure than the flowers themselves.

It is a fascinating occupation to take a winter bud to pieces on a sheet of white paper, and to recognise the many parts that go to its making. An ash bud which has been dissected in this way is shown in FIG. 2.

Large numbers of flowerless plants are at their best in winter, and this is particularly true of mosses and lichens. The rough-stalked feather-moss shown in PLATE 3 is now abounding in its delicate little fruiting capsules. It is one of the commonest of all our mosses, and can be found on banks, rocks, stones and dead wood almost everywhere.

The glittering feather-moss, which is a near relation of the rough-stalked species, is very attractive in January too. You will not find the *fruits* of this species until March or April, but its shining, feathery masses of yellowish-green foliage are now beautifying many a shady bank and woodland floor.

The yellow wall-lichen (PLATE 3) is another of these lowly plants which gives a touch of bright colour to the January country-side. You will find it not only on old walls, but on tree trunks, gates, palings, rocks, and cottage roofs in almost every part of the country.

17

CHAPTER II

FEBRUARY

BIRD LIFE IN FEBRUARY

UNLESS you have kept careful records over a number of years, you will probably be astonished at the large number of birds that plunge into their full song in February. If the weather is reasonably mild, you may expect to hear at least a score of species singing fairly regularly before the end of the month.

One of the most attractive of the new voices that February gives to us is the song of the blackbird (PLATE 6). You may, of course, hear occasional snatches of this song in January, but from about the middle of February onwards the bird is usually in fairly full song, and his extraordinarily mellow notes are different in quality from those of any other bird.

Now that the song-thrush, the mistle-thrush and the blackbird are all in full song, it is most interesting to compare the performances of these three fine singers. The blackbird differs from the song-thrush in having much shorter phrases of song and much longer intervals between them ; and his song is altogether more mellow and more leisurely than that of the mistle-thrush.

Other new-comers to the February choir are the chaffinch, the yellowhammer (PLATE 6), the corn bunting, the skylark, the coal tit, the marsh tit, the wren and the woodpigeon. All of these singers may, it is true, be heard at intervals during January, but it

PLATE 4.   FEBRUARY

WILD RABBIT.

Richard Morse, F.L.S.

WILD FRUITS IN WINTER.

Left: Ivy.   *Right*: Privet.

is not usually until February—perhaps even late in February—that you hear them performing their parts freely and regularly.

Another fascinating aspect of February bird life is the beginning of courtship, for already many birds are quite definitely displaying before their mates. Perhaps the most charming of all the courtships in birdland is that of the great crested grebes, which can be watched to perfection at this season. The way in which these

Fig. 3.—THE RAVEN.

handsome birds have extended their range in recent years should give joy to all lovers of Nature.

The courtship of the raven (Fig. 3) is another February event of great interest. The dives, the glides and the somersaults which the cock bird performs, often at crazy heights, show him to be not merely a lover, but a real master of the art of wingcraft. Ravens' nests are warmly lined with wool or rabbits' fur, and may often be found, complete with their blotched, bluish-green eggs, long before the end of the month.

C

Every rookery, too, is a place of special interest at this season, for the rooks, like their cousins the ravens, are very early in their courtships. Their visits to the rookery are now much more frequent than they were a month ago, and already they are busy at their old nests, sometimes reconstructing them, but often pulling them to pieces and starting all over again.

Towards the end of the month you may expect to see the beginning of spring migrations. Our first visitors from the south often arrive in February, and many of our resident birds leave their winter quarters for their nesting-grounds farther north.

ANIMAL LIFE IN FEBRUARY

Most of our hibernating mammals are still lying dormant in their hiding-places—the hedgehog curled up in the ditch-bottom, the dormouse, cold as death to the touch, in its tiny nest among the mosses, or under the earth, and the bats mostly hanging in old hollow trees, or in caves, barns or church towers.

Among those species that remain more or less wakeful throughout the winter, however, there is much activity. Most interesting of all, perhaps, are the squirrels, for instead of lying fast asleep, as they are often thought to do at this season, they are already building their nests—or dreys—in the forks of the trees.

A good deal, of course, depends upon the weather. There are reasons for believing that squirrels dislike high winds intensely, but they are certainly not afraid of the cold, for even if you do not see them actually bounding over the snow, you can often find their tell-tale footprints in it a little later (PLATE 6).

The rabbit (PLATE 4) is another mammal that begins its breeding

22

activities very early in the year, and not only may you find nests in February, but even litters of young ones. On light soils in warm districts, indeed, you can often see young rabbits in January.

The prowling carnivores are active too, but in another way, and a cross-country walk after a light fall of snow will provide speaking evidence of many a tragedy, in which a fox, a stoat or a weasel has played the leading part. Foot-writing in the snow, indeed, is one of the most interesting of Nature's manifold hieroglyphics (PLATE 6).

Frogs, toads and newts are usually still torpid in February if the winter is a severe one, but in milder seasons both frogs and toads are often abroad before the end of the month. Gilbert White recorded the croaking of frogs on the 25th of February, and the finding of frogspawn on the 28th. On this latter date, too, he recorded the appearance of the first toad.

Not often does February pass without giving us a glimpse of the first butterfly of the year. This is often a brimstone (PLATE 6), which a sunny day has awakened from its winter sleep, but occasionally it may be a small white—the earliest of all our butterflies to emerge from its pupal case.

The chrysalids of the small white and the large white butterflies are probably the most frequently observed of all chrysalids during the winter months. That of the large white is shown in PLATE 6 ; but when the wandering caterpillar comes to rest under a sheltering ledge, as it often does, the chrysalis is attached horizontally instead of vertically. Its colour, moreover, shows remarkable variations in relation to its environment—a fine example of protective coloration.

23

PLANT LIFE IN FEBRUARY

Plant life in general makes great strides in February, and fresh evidence of the coming spring can be seen almost every day. The leaves of the honeysuckle, the elder and the wild roses are already unfolding, and innumerable seedlings are jostling one another along the hedgebanks for a place in the sun.

Most conspicuous among the new blossoms which February brings are those of the lesser celandine and the coltsfoot—the one resembling a starry buttercup and the other a miniature dandelion. Both of them have large stores of food in underground organs, and it is upon those reserves that they draw for the making of their early flowers.

Much less conspicuous, but no less interesting, are the barren strawberry and the whitlow-grass (PLATE 6), both of which are usually in flower long before the end of the month. Their names, however, are singularly inappropriate, for the one is not a strawberry, and is certainly not barren, and the other is not in any way related to the grasses.

Yet at a first glance the so-called barren strawberry does resemble a miniature wild strawberry plant, and it is, in fact, often mistaken for one. It can easily be distinguished, however, by its notched petals and its absence of runners. Also the upper

KEY TO PLATE 6

1. Blackbird singing.	7. Whitlow-grass.
2. Brimstone butterfly on wing.	8. Pupa of large white butterfly.
3. Flowers of elm.	9. Footprints of stoat.
4. Flowers of alder.	10. Footprints of squirrel.
5. Yellowhammer singing.	11. Silvery thread-moss.
6. Barren strawberry.	12. Group of sulphur-tuft fungi.

PLATE 6.   FEBRUARY

FROM A FEBRUARY SKETCHBOOK.
(*See opposite page.*)

part of the flower-stalk does not become swollen, red and juicy, as in the true strawberry.

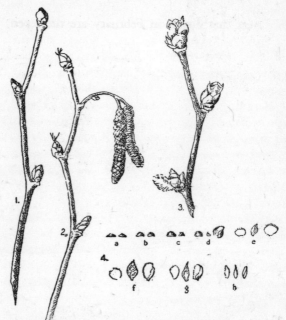

FIG. 4.—HAZEL TWIGS IN FEBRUARY.

1. Twig with winter buds.　　2. Twig with male and female flowers.
3. Twig with buds unfolding.　　4. Bud dissected, showing relation of scales to foliage leaves.
　　a, b, c. Outer scale leaves.　*d, e, f, g, h.* Inner scale leaves, each pair subtending a foliage leaf.

A good many of our trees and shrubs, too, are specially interesting just now. The male catkins of the alder (PLATE 6) are rather similar to those of the hazel (FIG. 4), but the alder's female flowers

26

are in the form of tiny cones, whereas those of the hazel look like small tufts of crimson hairs protruding from the tips of the buds. The two upper buds of the middle twig in Fig. 4 show these tufts clearly.

Other trees that flower in February are the aspen, the white poplar, the Lombardy poplar, the box and the elm (Plate 6). Elm flowers, unlike those of the alder and the hazel, normally contain both stamens and pistil in each separate flower, though sometimes you may find flowers from which the pistils are lacking.

The black fruits of the privet still stand out conspicuously along the bare hedgerows, for the birds seem to care but little for them so long as other fruits are available (Plate 5). Ivy berries, on the other hand, are eagerly sought by blackbirds and woodpigeons at this season. They are the latest of all our wild fruits to ripen, and March (or even April) may be far advanced before they are all cleared from their twigs (Plate 5).

Among the flowerless plants of February the pretty little silvery thread-moss is almost certain to attract attention. Its silver-green tufts and golden-brown capsules are very conspicuous on old roofs and wall-tops (Plate 6). More striking still is the sulphur-tuft fungus, whose bright colour beautifies many an old tree-stump even thus early in the year (Plate 6).

CHAPTER III

MARCH

BIRD LIFE IN MARCH

DURING March the great chorus of bird song continues to swell, not merely in volume, but in the number of singers. The score of performers that you listed during February will, indeed, probably grow to thirty before the end of the month ; and, given favourable weather, most of the thirty will be in fairly full song.

Chief among the new singers of March are the greenfinch, the goldfinch, the reed bunting, the meadow pipit, the wheatear and the chiffchaff. It is true that the first four of these can often be heard in February, but in that month their song tends to be broken and uncertain. In March, however, it becomes a regular and noticeable feature of the birds' daily chorus.

The yellowhammer's call for *A-little-bit-of-bread-and-no-cheese*, which is daily becoming more frequent, is one of the best-known bird songs in this country ; but the quaint little effort of its cousin, the reed bunting, is seldom noticed except by naturalists and anglers. It is, nevertheless, a song that can easily be distinguished from all others, and its recognition gives an added pleasure to any riverside ramble.

Another unmistakable song of March is that of the wheatear (PLATE 9). Nearly all the singers thus far mentioned are birds that stay in Britain throughout the winter. The wheatear, on the other hand, has only just arrived here from his winter home in the south, and he is therefore specially welcome as a real herald of the spring.

Following the wheatear very closely comes the chiffchaff—another early migrant. He, like the cuckoo, has gained his name from his song, and in woodland districts almost everywhere his clear piping of *Chiff-chaff-chiff-chiff-chaff* will be heard with scarcely a break from now—or at any rate from April—until the end of June.

Many of our sea birds, too, are on the move. Along the coast

FIG. 5.—PUFFINS IN FLIGHT.
The bird on the left is carrying fish for its young.

you can see such species as guillemots, razorbills and puffins gathering around their favourite nesting-sites. In autumn they leave the shore in large numbers for the open seas, but in spring, with unfailing regularity, they return.

The puffins, in particular, are worth careful watching, for they are unique among British birds. The way in which they carry fish to their young, the position of their feet in flight and other peculiarities should specially be noted (FIG. 5).

The courtships and matings of February will increase abundantly

D

during March ; and long before the end of the month the nests and eggs of thrushes, owls and other early builders will give a new interest to both woodland and hedgerow.

ANIMAL LIFE IN MARCH

Animal life, like bird life, shows an almost daily increasing activity during March, and signs of the coming spring can now be seen everywhere. It is interesting to notice, however, that even quite closely related species often show a considerable difference in their seasonal development.

March, for instance, is the month when the red deer drops his wonderful antlers—one of the most puzzling events, perhaps, in his whole life history—whereas those of the fallow deer (PLATE 7) are still firmly attached, and are likely to remain so until May.

It is in March, too, that you usually see the first signs of the quaint and amusing courtship antics of the hare (PLATE 9), whereas, as we saw last month, rabbits have been breeding since the beginning of the year.

And similarly, although you may frequently see great masses of frogspawn quite early in the month (PLATE 11), two or three weeks will probably pass before you catch a first glimpse of the toad's long necklaces of eggs, safely entangled among the rapidly developing water-weeds (PLATE 9).

Among insects, too, you may see similar differences. Thus the small white butterfly, as we have already seen, may emerge from its pupa as early as February, whereas the first of the large whites is not usually seen until the end of March, or more often, perhaps, until April.

PLATE 7. MARCH

WEASEL.

FALLOW DEER.

MOLE.

HEDGEHOG ASLEEP.

The hedgehog (PLATE 8) still sleeps soundly in the ditch-bottom, but his relatives, the moles and the shrews, have been active all through the winter. Both of these species fight fiercely among themselves in March or April—a sure sign that their breeding seasons have already begun (PLATE 8).

Foxes, too, are early breeders, and the first cubs are often born this month. Much the same also is true of stoats and weasels, which may pair as early as February. The weasel (PLATE 7) is an untiring enemy of the destructive field-vole, whose first litters of young may already be found in the nest (PLATE 12).

Many moths, butterflies and other insects, in addition to those already mentioned, are active during March. The red admiral, the small tortoiseshell, the comma and the peacock (PLATE 9), for instance, may all emerge from their hibernating quarters before the end of the month, and so also may queen wasps and humble-bees.

The March moth (PLATE 9), like the pale brindled beauty that we noted in January, is remarkable for the extraordinary difference between the sexes. The wingless female lays her eggs on the twigs of various kinds of trees and shrubs.

PLANT LIFE IN MARCH

The wild flowers of March include not only such universal favourites as the wood anemone, the marsh marigold, the lady's smock, the primrose, the sweet violet and the daffodil, but also a number of others which are more likely to be overlooked—the hairy bittercress, the moschatel, the ground ivy and the butter-bur, for example.

The field botanist finds interest as well as beauty in every one of

33

these plants. The primrose (PLATE 10), for example, bears flowers whose structure shows remarkable adaptations to insect pollination,

FIG. 6.—LADY'S SMOCK. HAIRY BITTERCRESS.

From Fitch's "British Flora" (Reeve, Ashford).

and the same is true of the violet (PLATE 9), while in the marsh marigold the sepals masquerade as petals, of which the flower has none (PLATE 9).

KEY TO PLATE 9

1. Chiffchaff.
2. Flowers of blackthorn.
3. March moth, male and female.
4. Peacock butterfly.
5. Grey cushioned grimmia in fruit.
6. Hare.
7. Sweet violet.
8. Flowers of sallow.
9. Marsh marigold.
10. Wheatear.
11. String of toadspawn.
12. Scarlet elf-cup fungus.

PLATE 9.   MARCH

FROM A MARCH SKETCHBOOK.
(*See opposite page.*)

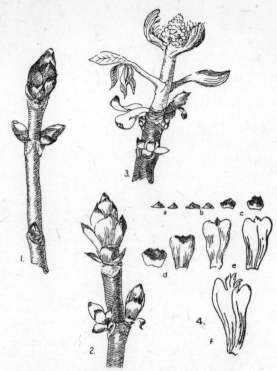

FIG. 7.—HORSE CHESTNUT TWIGS IN MARCH.

1. Twig with winter buds. 2. Twig with buds unfolding.
3. Terminal bud unfolded, showing inflorescence.
4. Series of bud-scales showing transition from scale to foliage leaf.
   a, b, c. Typical brown outer scales.
   d, e. Typical inner scales, pale green except at the exposed parts.
   f. Bud scale, forming petiole of a leaf.

The lady's smock and the hairy bittercress, which are shown side by side in FIG. 6, are very near relations. The white flowers

PLATE 10.

Sutton Palmer, R.I.

PRIMROSE TIME.

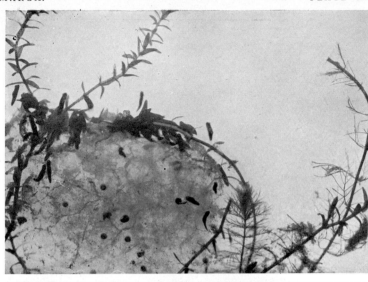

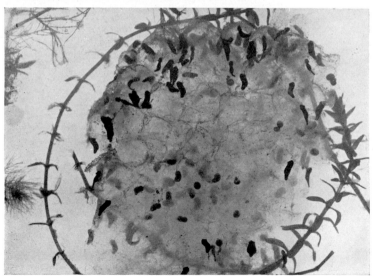

WHEN FROGS ARE YOUNG.

1. Photograph of frogspawn about a week old, showing the tadpoles emerging from the eggs. The tadpoles are now leaving the jelly-like mass for the clear water.

of the bittercress, however, are small and inconspicuous, whereas the large lilac ones of the lady's smock are beloved by country-folk everywhere. The leaves of both species have a cress-like taste, and are sometimes added to spring salads.

March, too, brings a number of our trees and shrubs into prominence. The blackthorn and the sallow, for example, may both be in flower well before the end of the month (PLATE 9), at any rate in mild seasons. The flowers of the sallow are the "palm" of country-folk, and are much used for Easter decorations.

Many other trees and shrubs, although not yet in flower, are rapidly unfolding their leaves. Some typical examples are the crab apple, the guelder-rose, the white willow, the birch, the dogwood and the sycamore. Most conspicuous of all, however, is the horse chestnut, whose opening buds are objects of great interest (FIG. 7).

March, like January and February, affords many opportunities for the study of mosses, lichens and other flowerless plants, of which vast numbers can now be found. The grey cushioned grimmia is a typical moss of the month. It grows abundantly on old walls, and forms neat little cushions of a greyish-green colour (PLATE 9).

The pretty little scarlet elf-cup—one of the most attractive of all our smaller fungi—should be sought in woods and ditches, where it can often be found growing on fallen hazel-sticks (PLATE 9). It is sometimes collected for table decoration.

39

CHAPTER IV

APRIL

BIRD LIFE IN APRIL

LAST month we noted the arrival of the two earliest summer visitors to this country—the wheatear and the chiffchaff—and next month we shall note the two latest of these visitors. It is, therefore, during the period between March and May that practically the whole of our remaining summer migrants reach these shores—a circumstance which gives to April an interest that is almost entirely its own.

This remarkable influx of migrants in April absolutely transforms the music of the countryside, for the great bulk of these birds are not merely singers, but singers that are bubbling over with energy. Almost every time you walk the fields, in fact, new voices greet you—voices that are, in many instances, marked by a peculiar sweetness and charm.

Quite early in the month, for instance, you may expect to hear such gifted singers as the willow warbler and the tree pipit. A little later will come the blackcap, and a little later still the white-throat, the sedge warbler, the wood warbler, the nightingale, the turtle dove and the garden warbler—and, of course, the cuckoo.

Although unfamiliar to most country-folk, the blackcap (PLATE 14) is a very accomplished vocalist. In some ways he is superior even to the nightingale. He has, for instance, no *harsh*

PLATE 12.   APRIL

FIELD VOLE PEEPING OUT OF ITS NEST.

DORMOUSE.

BROWN RAT.

notes at all, and he is an excellent mimic of several other fine singers, including the nightingale himself.

The songs of all these birds, and of a long list of others, are each quite distinct. A practised ear can recognise almost any one of them in an instant, and can gain great joy from so doing. The seemingly confused medley of the woodland or hedgerow can be analysed into its component parts, and each new-comer detected at the moment of its entry.

With all these new vocalists from abroad, and with so many of our own resident birds at the very height of their singing season, April shows almost as great an advance upon March as March itself showed upon February. Even among our relatively common birds it is fairly easy to list forty or more species which are now performing at their best.

The kind of singers that you hear, however, will depend to a considerable extent upon the region in which you listen, for many of our migrants settle down only in certain limited areas. But in that very fact lies one of the great attractions of April bird-watching, for it gives you an opportunity of seeing a number of interesting species which are now passing northwards on their way to their breeding-grounds.

The little-known ring-ousel, for example, is a bird of this kind. There is scarcely a county in England where you may not see it in April, but only in a few specially favoured regions will you find it during the summer (PLATE 14).

April, indeed, is so overflowing with bird activities of almost all kinds that the opportunities it offers to the bird-watcher are beyond count.

Movements on a large scale are in progress everywhere, for

E

not only are summer visitors arriving and winter visitors departing, but many even of our resident birds are seeking new quarters for the summer.

Nest-building, too, is now proceeding apace. The eggs of many species are already laid ; the young of others are already

FIG. 8.—LAPWING IN FLIGHT.

hatched. Often, too, the parent birds may be seen indulging in those peculiar performances known as " fancy " flights. The lapwing (FIG. 8) is a striking example, and its peculiar " drumming," similar to that of the snipe, is of special interest just now.

44

ANIMAL LIFE IN APRIL

In April, as in March, activities in the animal world become more pronounced every day. Mammals, reptiles, amphibians, fishes and a whole host of invertebrates will all provide entertainment for the careful watcher of their ways.

In the woods the squirrels, both red and grey (PLATE 14), may already have families of young ones in their dreys, and the parent animals may be seen carrying home food-materials of many kinds. They are particularly destructive to the buds of trees at this season, and hence are greatly disliked by the forester.

In the woods, too, the dormouse (PLATE 13) has at last awakened —or at least partly so, for he seems in no hurry to resume his full activities. His winter sleep is one of the longest, as well as one of the deepest, in the whole kingdom of mammals, and may last for fully six months out of the twelve.

In striking contrast to the dormouse is the brown rat (PLATE 13), which scorns hibernation, and which is not merely able to breed when only three months old, but which gives birth to an almost continuous succession of families the whole year through.

Hedgehogs and bats, as well as dormice, emerge from hibernation in April. Of special interest is that large bat known as the noctule, whose wing-expanse is often fourteen or fifteen inches. He flies much among high trees, though he frequently comes low enough for his shrill voice to be heard quite plainly.

Along the streamside the water voles are building their nests —a task in which they often show considerable ingenuity. The nest is not always in a burrow, but may be built on a specially

45

constructed platform of reeds, placed well above the surface of the water.

We noticed last month that toads are habitually later than frogs in their breeding activities ; and similarly, newts are usually considerably later than toads. They seldom emerge from hibernation until April, and the month may be far spent before you see them enclosing each egg separately in the fold of a leaf (PLATE 14).

In this country we have three species of newts, two of which are shown in FIG. 9. The third, known as the palmate newt, is scarce in our eastern counties, but commoner in the west. It is quite the smallest species of the three, and the male's hind feet become conspicuously webbed at this season.

April always brings a vast increase in the insect life of the countryside. Red admirals and small tortoiseshells are still on the wing ; peacocks and commas are still emerging from hibernation ; small whites (PLATE 14), large whites and green-veined whites are still emerging from their pupal cases ; and small coppers and hosts of others are now joining them.

A typical moth of the month is the appropriately named herald —attractive alike in form, colour and markings. It is first on the wing in August or September (PLATE 43), but later on goes into hibernation, and is then usually forgotten until its reappearance in early spring.

KEY TO PLATE 14

1. Flowers of wild cherry.
2. Blackcap singing.
3. Flowers of crab apple.
4. Early purple orchis.
5. Small white butterfly.
6. Seven-spot ladybird.
7. Fertile stem of field horsetail.
8. Cowslip.
9. Eggs of newt in leaves of water-weed.
10. Wall screw-moss.
11. Ring-ousel.
12. Grey squirrel.

PLATE 14.

FROM AN APRIL SKETCHBOOK.
(*See opposite page.*)

Very characteristic of April, too, are such familiar insects as the large, black St. Mark's fly, with its long, dangling legs, several

FIG. 9.—NEWTS IN APRIL.

(1) Crested newt, male.   (2) The same, female.   (3) Smooth newt, male.

kinds of early hoverflies and dragonflies, and the bloated, blue-black oil beetle, whose life history reads like a fairy-tale.

And lastly there are the ladybirds, which, in spite of their close relationship to the repulsive-looking oil beetle, are among the most attractive members of their race. The two-spotted and the seven-spotted species (PLATE 14) are just now emerging from their winter quarters, and will soon be playing havoc with the greenflies in the garden.

PLANT LIFE IN APRIL

With most of the wild flowers of March still flourishing, and with new ones being added almost every day, April is a very attractive month—and certainly a very busy one—for the field botanist.

Among the more familiar blossoms that may be expected during the month are those of the greater stitchwort, the greater celandine, the wild strawberry, the wild hyacinth, the wild arum, the early purple orchis, the cowslip and herb Robert. Illustrations of several of these will be found in PLATES, 14, 15 and 17.

The greater celandine (PLATE 17) grows commonly on hedgebanks near to human habitations, and may once have been cultivated as a medicinal herb. It is a member of the poppy family, and is in no way related to the lesser celandine, which is a relative of the buttercups.

The early purple orchis (PLATE 14) grows in association with the wild hyacinths in the woods, and is the first of our native orchids to come into blossom. It has an extraordinarily ingenious mechanism for ensuring the cross-pollination of its flowers—a process described in illuminating detail in Darwin's famous volume on the fertilisation of orchids.

Other interesting woodland plants of the month are the toothwort (a parasite), the woodsorrel (a sensitive plant), the wood crowfoot, or goldilocks (a small-flowered buttercup) and the wood spurge, which is a near relation of the very common sun spurge of our gardens.

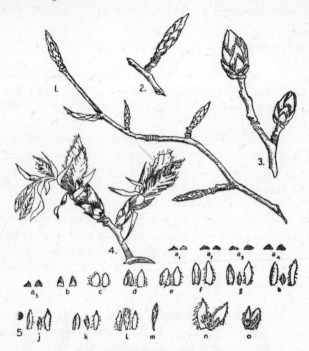

FIG. 10.—BEECH TWIGS IN APRIL.

1. Twig with winter buds.
2. Early stage in growth of bud.
3. Early stage in growth of a flowering bud.
4. Unfolding of winter buds.
5. Bud dissected, showing relation of bud scales to foliage leaves.

a_1, a_2, a_3, a_4, a_5. The first series of five pairs of scales, which are brown and coriaceous.
b, c, d, e, f. The second series of five pairs of scales, which are pale green and membranous.
g, h, j, k, l. The third series of scales enfolding foliage leaves.
m. Leaf which occupies the centre of the bud and is rolled into a cylinder.
n. A pair of scales enclosing leaf and staminate inflorescence.
o. A pair of scales enclosing leaf and pistillate inflorescence.

HERB ROBERT.

WOOD HORSETAIL.
Two fertile stems are shown on the left, and a barren one on the right.

Trees and shrubs everywhere are now almost scurrying into leaf and blossom. The alder, the aspen, the beech, the elm, the gorse, the holly, the lime, the maple, the oak, the white poplar and the yew are only a few of those whose buds may be watched unfolding during the month.

In FIG. 10 the buds of the beech are shown in various stages of development, together with the component parts of a dissected bud. It should be noted that the buds which contain flowers are much stouter than those which contain leaves only (compare Nos. 2 and 3 in the illustration).

Among the tree blossoms of April, those of the crab-apple and the wild cherry stand out conspicuously (PLATE 14), for they are some of the most beautiful of the year. But the flowers of the ash, the barberry, the birch, the holly, the oak and the sycamore may frequently also be found during the month.

Many of our flowerless plants, too, reach an interesting stage in April. The fertile stems of the field horsetail, the wood horsetail and the great horsetail, for example, can all be found this month (PLATES 14 and 16). The great horsetail is the largest British species, and may reach a height of six feet or more.

The wall screw-moss (PLATE 14) also fruits in April, and so does the pretty little apple-moss. The former grows chiefly on old walls, and the latter on dry banks, while in damp, shady places you can find large patches of the broad-leaved liverwort—now also in fruit.

CHAPTER V

MAY

BIRD LIFE IN MAY

JUST as we can think of April as the great month for observing the coming of our summer migrants, so can we think of May as the opening month of the grand season of nests and eggs and young ; for although there are some very early nesters, and also some very late ones, the great majority of our birds are either building or brooding in May.

It is especially at this season that you see the great value of the sober plumage of many female birds when compared with their mates, for it often needs a keen eye to detect them when they are brooding their eggs or young. Often, too, you may come across magnificent examples of natural camouflage—as in the case of the sitting pheasant, for example (PLATE 19).

The coming of so many young birds opens up an immense field for study and delight, as well as for camera work, painting and sketching. Some typical examples of such work are given in PLATES 18, 20 and 22, and also in FIG. 11 ; but the possibilities are infinite, and few other pictures of bird life have quite the same charm as those that are made in these later days of the spring.

The feeding of young birds by their parents is always interesting to watch. The energy shown by the parent birds needs to be observed with care to be fully appreciated, for the appetite of many nestlings appears to know no bounds. A pair of blue tits,

PLATE 17.   APRIL

THE GREATER CELANDINE.

C. F. Newall

Richard Morse, F.L.S.

YOUNG GREAT TIT.

for example, have been seen to take no fewer than two thousand caterpillars and other small prey to their family in one single day.

Nor does the interest cease when the young leave the nest. There is something peculiarly appealing about the gaping mouth, the entreating voice and the shivering wings of a hungry young bird ; and one is scarcely surprised to see other birds, as well as

FIG. 11.—YOUNG THRUSHES.

the parents, giving food in such cases—as when a robin, for instance, responds to the vigorous entreaties of a young thrush.

The great influx of summer migrants, which was so conspicuous in April, has now almost ceased. It is true that such birds as the swift and the nightjar, which are always late arrivals, may not be seen in some parts until May, but they are really April visitors, nevertheless.

Later still, however, are the red-backed shrike and the spotted

57

flycatcher, for although these birds may begin to arrive at the end of April, or even earlier than that, it is not until May is here that the main arrival takes place.

Although these two birds have but little to offer in the way of song, each is uniquely interesting in its ways of life—the shrike for its strange habit of impaling its prey on thorns, and the flycatcher for its oft-repeated sallies for insects from its chosen perch. Both birds are shown in PLATE 23.

But May, like April, in addition to all its other attractions, is a great month of song—the greatest, in fact, in all the twelve. Such birds as the whinchat, the garden warbler, the wood warbler and the turtle dove, which sang only intermittently in April, are now in really full song, as indeed are most of our other birds which can be classed as singers.

Such is the case, at any rate, in the early part of the month. Towards the end, however, a careful ear will detect changes. Family cares are increasing daily, with the inevitable result that song will diminish, both in frequency and intensity, as June draws steadily nearer.

The mistle-thrush affords a typical example of this waning song. In January, as we noticed, he came steadily into the choir, becoming more and more prominent as the weeks passed. Throughout February, March and April he was at his best, and even in early May you can detect no falling off. But always, before the end of the month, you begin to miss his loud challenge from the high tree-tops.

Much the same, too, is true of the starling. Although he is a bird which has no really silent month in all the twelve, he always sings less regularly as the summer advances, and it is usually in the middle of May that you begin to miss the customary fullness of his song.

Another interesting aspect of bird life in May is the number of unsolved problems that it presents. With all our prying into the cuckoo's domestic affairs, for example, there is still much that escapes us, and the veriest amateur may be fortunate enough at any time to witness events that throw new light upon the vagaries of this peculiarly wayward bird.

Very puzzling, too, are the swifts and the nightjars, both of which are certain to attract attention during the present month. In the dusk of the evening you may see parties of swifts circle upwards until they are lost to sight. Do these birds sleep on the wing, or do they descend to their roosting-places when darkness has fallen ? There seems to be no positive answer to this question.

And a similar mystery surrounds the familiar clapping sound which is so often made by the nightjar when in flight. You may sometimes hear a score or more of these so-called claps in quick succession ; but could such a sound really be made by the mere contact of such soft objects as a nightjar's wings ? Here, again, there is no adequate answer.

ANIMAL LIFE IN MAY

It is not only among birds that May is largely a month of nurseries and young, for in the animal world as a whole the same truth holds good. One of the great charms of the countryside to-day, in fact, lies in the many glimpses we get of the new young lives that now throng the fields and woodlands.

In early May, for instance, we may expect to see fox cubs

exploring the new world that lies outside their "earth." They are handsome little creatures, and as playful as puppies. They are, however, already suspicious of man, and you must approach them very warily if you wish not to disturb them in their games.

The habit of foxes to hunt chiefly after dusk is not really a natural habit of the species, but one that has been forced upon it by the persistent persecution of man—the fox's one great enemy. This is shown plainly by the obvious delight of the cubs as they romp and play in the first warm sunshine of the spring.

Very charming, too, at any rate in appearance, are the families of young stoats, which come abroad with their mothers in May or June. You may see them all together, sometimes, squirming in the grasses, and peeping at you with their dark little eyes, as they learn their first lessons in the great art of hunting.

Young weasels, young badgers, young otters, young moles, young shrews, young hedgehogs, young rabbits, young hares, young squirrels, young rats, young mice and young voles are a few of the other infants that can be found in the fields in May, though not all of them will yet have left their nurseries.

The different species of animals often differ widely in regard to the development of the young at the time of their birth. Thus baby rabbits, in keeping with their underground life, are both blind and naked, whereas baby hares, with no burrows for protection, have open eyes and furry coats, and are very soon able to fend for themselves.

The common shrew (PLATE 23) is a specially interesting little animal from May onwards. It breeds freely from now until November, but there is still much that is obscure in its life history. It is said often to die during thunderstorms—perhaps from shock—

PLATE 19.   MAY

Photos: Richard Morse, F.L.S.

THREE FIR-RAPES.

PEN PHEASANT SITTING.

Roland Green

BARN OWL ABOUT TO FEED YOUNG.

ANIMAL LIFE: MAY

and towards the end of summer, as we shall see in a later chapter, shrews die in immense numbers without any apparent cause at all.

Of special interest at this season, too, is the long-eared bat (PLATE 23), for the mother is now—or soon will be—carrying her solitary infant with her wherever she goes. It clings tightly to her fur, and feeds at her breast as she chases the moths in the twilight.

In May all our amphibians are passing through some of the most interesting stages of their life histories. The edible frog may only just be laying her eggs ; the newts are still laying theirs ; and the gradual transformation of the earlier tadpoles into adult forms is a piece of Nature's magic that never grows stale.

Most of the insect kingdom, too, is pulsating with activity. New-comers among the butterflies include such common species as the wall, the small heath, the pearl-bordered fritillary, the common blue, the green hairstreak and the orange-tip (PLATE 23) ; and a number of beautiful hawk-moths are now emerging from their pupal cases.

Then there are the mayflies (PLATE 23)—those fragile insects which grovel in the mud for years for the sake of a few hours of aerial joy. Special watch should be kept for their remarkable evening dances towards the end of the month—especially along slow-flowing streams.

Although we usually do not think much about wasps at this season, it is now that they are beginning to build their nests— some of the most extraordinary structures, surely, in the length and breadth of the countryside (FIG. 12).

It is important to remember that the nests of all our social wasps —in spite of the fact that a single nest may produce well over twenty thousand individuals during the summer—are begun by a solitary insect, working all alone, for it is only the young

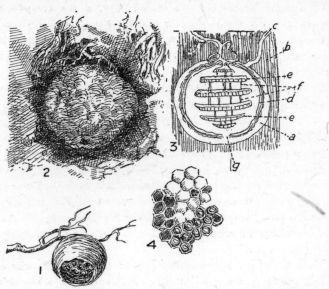

FIG. 12.—THE MAKING OF A WASPS' NEST.

1. Nest of wasp. Early stage (⅓ natural size).
2. Nest of wasp, showing its attachment to roots, its flaky covering, and the entrance at the bottom.
3. Diagram of section of nest :
   - (*a*) Cavity in the ground.   (*b*) Soil.
   - (*c*) Entrance to nest from the surface of the ground.
   - (*d*) Covering of nest consisting of several layers.
   - (*e*) Combs (space between the combs exaggerated).
   - (*f*) Pillars of wasp " paper " to which the combs are attached.   (*g*) Entrance into nest.
4. Part of a comb showing cells occupied by larvæ, others enclosing pupæ and covered, and some empty.

" queens " that survive the winter. One of these is shown, fast asleep, in PLATE 3.

PLATE 21. MAY

SWEET WOODRUFF.

Roland Gree

KINGFISHER AND YOUNG.

Other pieces of Maytime magic among the insects are the intricate tailoring activities of the caddis-worms, the emergence of the puss moth from its hard cocoon on the tree-trunk, the formation of oak-apples and currant galls, and the merry chirping of the field crickets.

These last insects appear to be much scarcer to-day than they were in years gone by. Gilbert White said of them that " they chirp all night as well as day," and that " in hot weather, when they are most vigorous, they make the hills echo."

PLANT LIFE IN MAY

Both the bird and the animal kingdoms, as we have already seen, abound in energy during May, and a similar expression of abundant vitality can be seen also in the great kingdom of plants. Vegetation everywhere now, in fact, is attaining such vast proportions that a more or less systematic approach is essential if you wish to avoid the bewilderment to which such an immense mass of material may well give rise.

Perhaps the best plan is to visit a number of well-defined regions in turn, to look in a broad, general way at the characteristic plants of those regions, and then to devote any time that may still be available to a more detailed study of some of the individual species.

A start, for instance, might be made with woods and hedgerows, for the vegetation of a hedgerow is very similar to that which characterises the margin of a wood.

In the wood itself many of the plants of March and April, and some even of January and February, will still be flourishing, but a number of new-comers are bound to attract your attention.

The strange little fir-rape (PLATE 19), for instance, is pale yellow instead of green, and the sweet woodruff (PLATE 21) catches your eye at once with its rings of narrow leaves and its pure white, starry flowers. Conspicuous, too, are such plants as wood sanicle, twayblade and herb paris, while under your feet is the attractive little swan's-neck thread-moss, with its nodding capsules of spores (PLATE 23).

Then again, a number of our trees and shrubs, both of woodland and hedgerow, have made good progress since last month. Not only the elder and the hawthorn (PLATE 23) have now opened their flowers, but perhaps the guelder-rose too, and the spindle-tree and the maple and the beech, while some of the willows may already be scattering their feathery seeds.

Flowers of quite a different type will be found in meadows, pastures and grassy places in general. Here there may be great sheets of yellow buttercups, or dandelions, or bird's-foot trefoils, with varying quantities of milkwort, fairy flax, tormentil, eye-bright, yellow-rattle or the big oxeye daisy.

The sweet vernal grass (PLATE 23) is of special interest because of the sweet fragrance that it gives off while drying ; and the flower-heads of the dandelion will tell a fascinating floral story with the help of a pocket-lens (FIG. 13). Each separate floret is a flower in miniature, with its own highly specialised mechanism for ensuring effective pollination.

In some pastures those deep-green circles known to country-folk as fairy-rings may be seen, and in them at this season you may find the fairy-ring champignon (PLATE 23), which is often—though not always—responsible for their formation.

No less interesting than the May-time woodlands and grasslands are the May-time water-sides and marshes, where, once again, a quite different type of vegetation will be found.

In the actual water itself the very attractive little water buttercup (PLATE 23) often grows so profusely that it completely covers the surface of either pond or stream. A typical group of aquatic

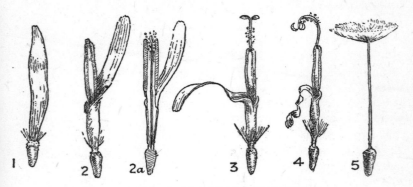

FIG. 13.—HOW A DANDELION FLORET DEVELOPS.

Stages in the development of a floret.

1. Floret in bud.
2. Floret showing anthers united to form a tube. The stigma-lobes, still closed, are appearing at the top.
2a. Floret at the same stage, but in longitudinal section, showing the pollen which the anthers have shed within the tube and which is being pushed up by the hairy style. Insects may carry the pollen away.
3. Floret in which the stigma-lobes have expanded and are ready for pollination by an insect.
4. Floret in which the stigma-lobes have curled back and may touch some pollen grains, thus bringing about self-pollination.
5. Fruitlet with pappus.

plants is shown in PLATE 24, though not all of these will be in flower until a little later in the year.

Some other characteristic plants of this same region in May are the ragged robin, with its deeply-cut, rose-coloured petals, the water forget-me-not, with its yellow-eyed flowers of heavenly blue, and the lesser spearwort—a plant which is often passed by as a buttercup, but whose simple, uncut leaves distinguish it in a moment.

There are, of course, a number of other well-defined regions that are worth a visit at this season. Some of these, such as a rocky mountain-side or a sandy seashore, may be truly natural regions ; others, such as the ploughlands of the farmer, may be wholly artificial ones. Each of them, however, carries a flora that has interesting characteristics of its own.

Outstanding among the plants of the cornfield, for instance, are those species which, in spite of their widespread abundance, are really aliens—the corn poppy (PLATE 28) and the corn marigold, for example. Such plants can flourish only so long as the plough prepares the way for them, and they would mostly disappear from our flora if our fields and gardens were allowed to run wild.

KEY TO PLATE 23

1. Flowers of hawthorn.	5. Flowers of elder.	9. Swan's-neck thread-moss.
2. Orange-tip butterfly.	6. Sweet vernal grass.	10. Water buttercup.
3. Long-eared bat.	7. Mayflies in flight.	11. Common shrew.
4. Red-backed shrike.	8. Spotted flycatcher.	12. Fairy-ring toadstools.

PLATE 23.

MAY

FROM A MAY SKETCHBOOK.
(*See opposite page.*)

CHAPTER VI

JUNE

BIRD LIFE IN JUNE

IN May we saw the grand opening of the nesting season : in June we shall watch its magnificent culmination. Everywhere to-day the countryside abounds in new life. First broods, second broods, and in some cases third broods, are now all playing their parts— or soon will be playing their parts—in the great summer pageant of bird life (FIG. 14).

The observations of parent birds and their young which we began last month can, during the present month, be extended in many directions. The possibilities here, in fact, are illimitable; and there is perhaps no other aspect of bird study that can be more entrancing than this, whether to amateur or to expert.

Outstanding among the sounds of June are the many new voices that you hear in every woodland and hedgerow. Unlike the new voices that we noted in the earlier months of the year, however, they are not in the form of songs, for June brings us no new songs at all. They are the almost incessant calls of the young birds to their parents, and the special twitterings, chatterings and calls of the parent birds to their young.

It is interesting to try to interpret some at least of these multitudinous calls of the June countryside, for they undoubtedly serve more than one important purpose in the evolution of bird life.

Very often, of course, the call of the young bird is quite definitely a hunger-call, and the parent undoubtedly recognises it as such. But some young birds utter also a note of contentment, or a cry of fear, or a wail of anxiety, or even, in spite of their almost utter helplessness, an unmistakably menacing note in the face of an enemy.

FIG. 14.—WREN WITH FOOD FOR YOUNG.

You will notice, too, that the calls of the parent birds change with the season. They do not use for their children the same language that they use for their mates. You can distinguish in a moment, for instance, the warning note of the song-thrush, a note which holds its threatened babe motionless and invisible, or nearly so, until the danger has passed.

73

Of special interest to the student of evolution is the fact that the behaviour of young birds varies with their environing conditions. Thus young birds in open nests do not, as a rule, call for food. No matter how keen their pangs of hunger may be, they must bear those pangs in silence, since to cry aloud would almost certainly betray to some prowling enemy the whereabouts of their defence-less bodies.

The young of such birds as the owls and the starlings, on the other hand, being reared mainly in *enclosed* places, have little to fear from prowling enemies. They can, therefore, in most cases, give vent to their feelings without endangering their lives—or at any rate without seriously endangering them.

Now that our three species of swallow-birds, and maybe their young ones too, are all in the air together, there will be many opportunities for observing their similarities and their differences, not merely in form and colour, but in their manner of flight and their habits too (PLATE 28).

The resemblance of the swift to the swallow does not, of course, indicate any kind of *blood* relationship between these two birds. It does, however, afford a fine example of what the biologist calls " convergence "—the evolution, that is, from quite different origins, of similar adaptations in relation to similar conditions of life.

Our two final notes concerning the bird life of June must be very brief ones. Migration, more markedly perhaps than in any other month of the year, is practically at a standstill ; and bird song, from its remarkable crescendo of last month, is noticeably dwindling day by day. To both of these topics, however, we shall return next month.

PLATE 24.   JUNE

SOME PLANTS OF THE POND.
1. Great Water Plantain.   2. Yellow Waterlily.   3. Water Buttercup.
4. Arrowhead.   5. Water Soldier.

75

NEST OF LEAFCUTTER BEE.

The photograph shows three series of cells arranged in borings in the wood.

ANIMAL LIFE IN JUNE

The steady multiplication of wild animal life which we noticed in May does not by any means end with the month itself, so that June also, at any rate so far as the mammals are concerned, is largely a month of family activities—and therefore a very interesting month.

The young of the red deer, the fallow deer and the roe deer, for example, may all be seen at this season by those who are fortunate enough to have such animals within easy access, and many pretty little instances of parental affection can be witnessed.

For the hind is a brave and attentive mother. You may see her gently pat her fawn with her hoof, or push it with her nose, to teach it to lie flat while she is away. And if it calls for help, she will face many a fierce foe in its defence.

In June, too, if you silently watch a badger's "earth" after sunset, you may have the joy of seeing not merely the parent animals, but the cubs too, emerge from their burrows. Like so many other young creatures, badger cubs are fond of play. Their games, however, are strangely silent, for any noise would at once betray their whereabouts.

If you are doubtful as to whether a wood is tenanted by these unusually interesting animals, there are various daytime observations that can easily be made. You can, for example, usually find their footprints, which are quite different from those of any other British animal ; or you can look for their well-trodden runway just outside the "earth" ; or you can search for their unmistakable hairs among the litter which they remove from their dens.

H

June is also one of the best months for watching the bats, for all our native species are now on the wing, and many may be carrying their young. Owing to their habit of flying mainly in dusk or darkness, they are not easy to identify, though some of them have characteristics with which one soon becomes familiar.

The noctule, for instance, flies high in the early evening, often joining the swifts before they retire. The long-eared bat is a lover of trees, and often takes its food from their leaves, sometimes alighting in order to do so. And the water bat flies low over rivers and lakes, taking insects from the surface of the water, or drinking as it flies.

Along the riverside the first young water voles may now be expected. Even while still quite small, they take readily to the water, and swim and dive with an instinctive cleverness that is most interesting to watch.

Young dormice, too, usually make their appearance in June. At first they are blind and naked, but are soon able to leave the nest. Even when fully grown, they can be distinguished from their parents by their greyer coats.

In streams and rivers, young fishes now abound, including those of the bullhead, or miller's thumb (PLATE 28)—a fish which, like the stickleback, prepares a nest for its eggs—or at any rate an apology for one. And snails and slugs in seemingly endless variety can be found wherever there are leaves to be eaten (PLATE 28).

The number of insects that are now on the wing—and on foot —is also bewilderingly great. There are mayflies and dragonflies, moths and butterflies, gallflies and sawflies, gnats and midges, bugs and beetles, and countless thousands of ants and wasps and bees.

PLATE 26.   JUNE

Richard Morse, F.L.S.

BEE ORCHIDS.

THE LARGE WILD CONVOLVULUS.

The lacewing-fly is remarkable for its gauzy wings, its golden eyes and its long-stalked eggs. The beautiful cinnabar moth,

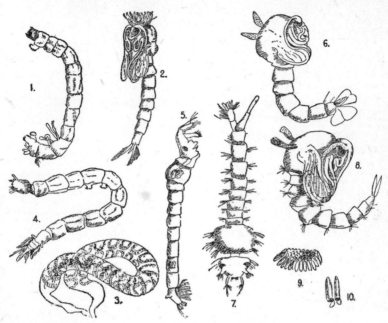

FIG. 15.—GNATS AND MIDGES.

1. Larva of *Chironomus*, known as "bloodworm."
2. Pupa of *Chironomus*.
3. Egg rope of *Chironomus*.
4. Larva of *Dixa*.
5. Phantom larva (*Corethra*).
6. Pupa of phantom fly.
7. Larva of gnat (*Culex*).
8. Pupa of gnat.
9. Egg raft of gnat.
10. Two eggs (more highly magnified) showing the opening by which the larva escapes.

with its vermilion hind-wings, should be sought on downs and heaths where ragwort grows, for it is chiefly on this plant that its orange-and-black caterpillars feed. Both of these insects are shown on PLATE 28.

Of very special interest at this season is the work of the leaf-cutter bees, some of which so frequently cut semicircular pieces from rose leaves for the lining of their cells. You can find examples of their remarkable upholstery not only in old wood (PLATE 25), but also in dry banks, in the burrows of earthworms and in a host of other places.

The fascinating life histories of gnats and midges can be studied to perfection in June, not merely in the garden water-butt, but in stagnant water almost everywhere—including especially that which collects in the hollows of old trees. A selection of typical eggs, larvae and pupae is shown in FIG. 15.

PLANT LIFE IN JUNE

The rich abundance of plant life that was characteristic of May will be richer still in June, and here again, therefore, only brief glances at a few special regions will be possible in these notes.

Looking first at a typical piece of woodland, we shall notice that the abundance here is of leaf rather than of flower. Most flowers are lovers of sunshine, and as soon as the great canopy of the trees spreads itself across the wood, the spring-time loveliness of the woodland flowers fades rapidly away.

KEY TO PLATE 28

1. Swallow in flight.	5. Corn poppy.	9. Common hair-moss.
2. House martin in flight.	6. Cinnabar moth.	10. Edible boletus.
3. Flowers of sweet chestnut.	7. Lacewing-fly.	11. Common black slug.
4. Agrimony.	8. Field rose.	12. Bullhead, or miller's thumb.

PLATE 28.

JUNE

FROM A JUNE SKETCHBOOK.
(*See opposite page.*)

There are, however, a few of our wild-flowers that are able to flourish in shady woods at this season—the beautiful butterfly orchid, for example—and where the shade is not too dense you may find such interesting and attractive little plants as the yellow

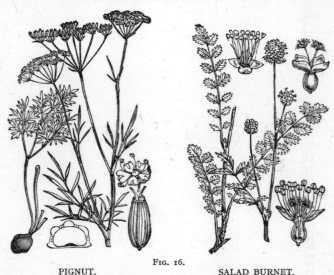

FIG. 16.

PIGNUT.   SALAD BURNET.
From Fitch's " British Flora," (Reeve, Ashford).

pimpernel, the creeping Jenny, the yellow cow-wheat and the pignut (FIG. 16).

With the fading of the great masses of early spring flowers, a number of flowerless plants, too, come into prominence in the wood, some typical examples being the polypody among the ferns, the edible boletus among the fungi, and the common

3.

C. F. Newall.

THREE INTERESTING FERNS.
1. Common Adder's-tongue. 2. Lesser Adder's-tongue. 3. Moonwort.

hair-moss—a veritable giant of its tribe (PLATES 28 and 30).

And one, at least, of the woodland trees—the sweet chestnut —is in flower in June (PLATE 28), while along the margins of the wood you may find such attractive blossoms as those of the dog rose, the field rose and the large white convolvulus (PLATES 27 and 28).

Turning now from the shady woodlands to the June meadows and pastures, we find an array of blossom that no other month can surpass. The grasses themselves are almost bewildering in their variety, and associated with them are such plants as clovers, vetches, bedstraws, knapweeds and cranesbills, together with countless May-time wild-flowers still in their prime.

The agrimony (PLATE 28), the salad burnet (FIG. 16) and the adder's-tongue fern (PLATE 29) attract relatively little attention to-day, but years ago they were all assiduously collected by country-folk for use in salads and medicines, while the moonwort (PLATE 29) was regarded as a veritable wizard of the vegetable kindgom.

By inland water-sides also there are many attractions in June, among which the meadowsweet stands out conspicuously, with its dense masses of creamy-white, fragrant flowers. The great water plantain (PLATE 24) is attractive, too, but its pale-lilac flowers are peculiarly delicate and very short-lived. In spite of its name, it is in no way related to the plantains of our fields and gardens.

But perhaps the most interesting of all aquatic plants just now is the bladderwort (FIG. 17). It has no roots at any period of its life, but by way of compensation is able to feed upon the minute animal life of the water in which it floats. The bladders from which its name is derived are traps of the most ingenious construction.

Finally, there are the June cornfields, now ablaze with scarlet

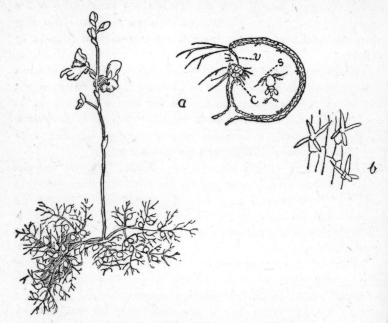

FIG. 17.—THE BLADDERWORT AND ITS TRAPS.
(*a*) Section of bladder, much magnified, showing (*s*) cyclops imprisoned in cavity, (*v*) valve closing the entrance, and (*c*) cushion upon which the valve rests. (*b*) Star-shaped cells from the inner surface of the bladder, much magnified.

corn poppies (PLATE 28), but the home, too, of a large number of tough and hardy little wild-flowers—all full of interest for the field botanist, but the despair of many a harassed farmer.

PLATE 31.

JULY

GOUTWEED.

SOME MOTHS OF THE GARDEN.

1. Humming-bird Hawk.
2. Scarlet Tiger.
3. Buff Ermine.
4. White Ermine.
5. Puss Moth.
6. Lackey.
7. Cabbage Moth.
8. Turnip Moth.
9. Heart and Dart.
10. Yellow Underwing.
11. Magpie, or Currant, Moth.

CHAPTER VII

JULY

Bird Life in July

AT the very beginning of July it is interesting to glance backwards at one's records, both on paper and in the memory, of bird song during May and June—records, that is, not merely of the species that could be heard singing, but also of the general character and frequency of their song.

A broad glance of that kind will usually bring to light some interesting facts. It will show, for example, that the outstanding feature of bird song in May was its remarkable fullness and regularity. Almost every bird that sings at all was then singing at its best ; and the great volume of the daily chorus was striking enough to capture the attention of the most casual observer.

And the early days of June were very similar to those of May —there was still an abundance of song everywhere. As the month wore away, however, a marked diminution, of which May had already given us a foretaste, began to show itself, not so much, perhaps, in the number of species that could be heard singing, as in the growing infrequency of their song.

In the first part of the month, for example, such birds as the linnet, the chaffinch, the greenfinch, the tree pipit, the nightingale, the wren and the cuckoo were all singing freely and fully, whereas in the latter part of the month it was the exception, rather than the rule, to hear them at their best.

And it is this gradual waning of bird song, now greatly accentuated, that characterises July. One after another the bulk of our best singers are either dropping out of the chorus altogether, or are making their songs dependent upon such uncertain factors as food supply, domestic cares and the vagaries of the weather. It is scarcely possible to find even half a dozen species that will give us of their best throughout July.

The woodpigeon, it is true, sings on with undiminished vigour,

FIG. 18.—THE DIPPER AT HOME.

and so also do the turtle dove (PLATE 33) and some of the buntings, at any rate until very late in the month. By that time, however, a marked general silence has usually settled down upon the countryside, and even the little dipper—one of the most persistent of singers—temporarily forgets his song, and contents himself with his remarkable activities in and under the water (FIG. 18).

Perhaps the most remarkable of the singers still left to us is the nightjar, whose almost uncanny, whirring song can be heard on most nights throughout the earlier part of the month. All our other night singers sing by day too, but only on very rare occasions will you hear the nightjar until after the sun has set.

There is no other British bird whose song could possibly be mistaken for that of the nightjar. It is a strange, churring sound, more like the distant throbbing of a motor-cycle than a bird's voice ; and although it has a peculiarly low, mellow pitch, it has remarkable carrying power. On quiet nights it can be heard fully half a mile away.

July, however, has many bird interests apart from bird song. Now that large numbers of young birds have grown to the size of their parents, there are many opportunities for comparing the plumage of youth with that of maturity, for there are often wide differences.

The bald face which is so very characteristic of the adult rook, for example, is entirely lacking in the young birds of the year. These immature rooks have bristled and feathered faces, and are consequently often mistaken for crows.

The young robin, too, is another bird which frequently causes confusion. Although very obviously a robin, it has no red breast, and for that reason is often taken to be a *hen* robin (PLATE 33). Everyone who has watched a pair of robins at nesting time, however, will know that *both* sexes have red breasts when they are mature.

The study of juvenile plumages, indeed, is a fascinating one, not merely for the bird-watcher, as such, but for the biologist too. It throws much light, for example, upon bird relationships and the story of evolution, and it opens up a score of subtle and intricate problems which cannot even be mentioned here, but which are, nevertheless, well worthy of the attention of every serious student of bird life.

Last month we noted the almost complete absence of anything that could be called migration, for at midsummer there was little need for extensive travel. During July, however, with so many young birds of the year now fully grown, a number of migratory movements are certain to attract attention, particularly among those species known as passage migrants, or birds of passage.

The whimbrel may be taken as a typical example of such birds. Every year, in early spring, it flies northwards from Africa, vast numbers passing along our shores on their way, perhaps, to Shetland or northern Europe. And every year, from July onwards, it flies southwards again, often staying for a while at various places *en route*.

These early migrations mark very clearly the turn of the year, for even in the scorching July sun they speak in no uncertain terms of the approach of autumn. They are, in a word, the beginning of the annual mass-movement to the south—the grand trek that will be of such absorbing interest to every lover of birds during the next three months.

ANIMAL LIFE IN JULY

In July, as in June, the land, the air and the water teem with animal life in all its countless forms. Many of the young creatures

---

KEY TO PLATE 33

1. Spray of wild clematis, in flower.
2. Flowers of lime tree.
3. Couchgrass.
4. Harebell.
5. Turtle dove.
6. Magpie moth.
7. Blunt-leaved bogmoss in fruit.
8. Female glow-worm.
9. Young robins.
10. Zebra spider.
11. Common centipede.
12. Wood-witch fungus.

PLATE 33.

JULY

FROM A JULY SKETCHBOOK.
(*See opposite page.*)

that we noted in earlier months are already as large as their parents, but others are still arriving.

In some cases the new-comers are children of second—or perhaps even of third—litters. Rabbits, for example, breed regularly from February to September, and irregularly through the winter ; and young rats are far too common in every month of the year.

The long-tailed field mouse (PLATE 39) is another prolific little animal. It often becomes a mother before it is half a year old ; and litter follows litter through all the summer months.

The mole, on the other hand, having far fewer enemies, can keep up its numbers by producing only one family—and that not a large one—in the course of the year. The young are born chiefly in May, but they are very helpless babies, and are seldom seen abroad until late in June or early in July.

And it is much the same with the hedgehog, so marvellously protected from most of its enemies by its coat of sharp spines. Young hedgehogs, as we have already noticed, can be found occasionally in May, though it is not usually until July that you see them out with their mother in the dusk of the late evening. Sometimes, however, the hedgehog produces a second litter of young in the autumn.

The pipistrelle—the commonest and the smallest of our British bats—is even less prolific than either mole or hedgehog, and is another late breeder. Its " family "—in this country at any rate —seldom or never exceeds one in number, and it is during the present month that that solitary infant is carried by its mother in her evening flights.

Last month we noted some of the indications that mark the presence of badgers in a wood. As the summer advances, you may expect further evidence in the shape of looted wasps' nests. The wasps probably fiercely resent the night attack upon their cities, but their efforts in self-defence appear of little avail, for the destruction goes on with systematic thoroughness every summer.

An interesting sight by the July streamside is the emergence of young frogs and toads from the water in which they have spent the whole of their early lives. Sometimes they are so numerous in the damp grass that it is almost impossible to walk without treading upon them ; and their mortality rate at this season must often be appallingly high.

July, too, is a good month for observing the ways of our native lizards, for they love to bask on warm, sunny banks, and to snap up the unfortunate insects that come within their range. The so-called blindworm is a lizard without legs. Although absolutely harmless, it is, on account of its snake-like appearance, woefully persecuted by those who are unaware of its real nature (PLATE 38).

Another lover of July sunshine is the very distinctive little zebra spider—or jumping spider, as it is sometimes called (PLATE 33). Its movements on a sunny wall are well worth watching. It pounces upon its prey with a mighty spring, and cleverly ensures its own safety by means of a drag-rope of fine silk.

The common centipede (PLATE 33), on the other hand, is a lover of darkness, and scurries into a place of shelter as fast as its many legs will carry it. The mother centipede's habit of disguising her eggs with earth is explained, perhaps, by the father centipede's apparently irresistible desire to eat them as soon as they are laid.

The insect life of the year is now probably at its zenith. In species and in individuals alike its numbers are beyond count and the month will slip away before we have had time even to glance at more than a tiny fraction of the hordes that now invite attention.

Dragonflies, in particular, will amply repay anyone's careful

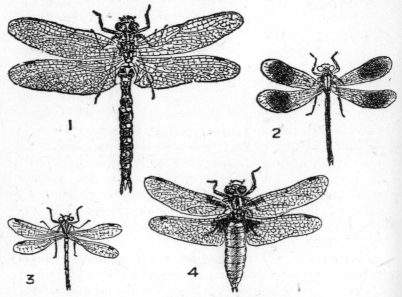

FIG. 19.—FOUR TYPES OF DRAGONFLIES.

1. Hawker dragonfly (*Aeshna cyanea*).   2. Demoiselle (*Agrion virgo*).
3. Blue-needle dragonfly (*Coenagrion puella*).   4. Broad-bodied dragonfly (*Libellula depressa*).

study. The emergence of the winged insect from the sluggish nymph is a never-to-be-forgotten sight ; and few creatures, surely, can claim a greater command of the air. One is, indeed, little surprised to learn that some of them—like some of the

PLATE 34.

JULY

HENBANE.

C. F. Newall

birds—are true migrants, and that some—even excelling the birds —can fly backwards as well as forwards. Four typical forms are shown in FIG. 19.

The moths figured in PLATE 32, with the exception of the scarlet tiger, are quite common ones, and most of them can be found in or around the garden during July. The magpie, which is included also in PLATE 33, is one of the most variable of all our moths. It often lays its eggs on currant and gooseberry bushes, and its caterpillars may then become a very serious pest.

Yet another interesting July insect is the glow-worm (PLATE 33). Her cold, green light has long been the envy of human lamp-makers, for even the most efficient of our own lighting systems dissipate the greater part of their energy in more or less useless heat.

PLANT LIFE IN JULY

Although the woods in July have lost most of their sweet freshness of the spring, there are many compensations, and one of the greatest of these is provided by the beautiful rosebay willow-herb, whose tall spires of rosy flowers have won for it a place in many a cottage garden.

Very characteristic of the July woodland, too, or at any rate of its immediate vicinity, are such plants as the wood betony, the greater skullcap, the musk mallow and the enchanter's nightshade —all of them now in full flower. The last-named is a near relation of the rosebay willowherb, and is not in any way connected with our other nightshades—the deadly, the woody and the black.

Among the flowerless plants of the woodland that are specially

K

worth noting at this season are many of our native ferns, including the male fern, the lady fern, the hard fern (PLATE 37) and the brake, or bracken, all of which are now producing their myriads of microscopic spores.

It should be noticed that the hard fern, unlike the other species mentioned, produces fronds of two kinds—one barren, the other fertile. The beautiful parsley fern (PLATE 35) behaves in a similar way, but that is a plant of the mountain-side.

Less attractive, perhaps, though no less interesting, are a number of fungi, mosses and other lowly plants, two examples of which —the wood-witch fungus and the blunt-leaved bogmoss—are shown in PLATE 33.

The common lime tree is not a native of this country, but is widely planted, and calls for mention here because of its deliciously fragrant blossoms. The wild clematis, also now in flower, is a climbing shrub of woodland margins and hedgerows, and is often abundant in counties south of the Wash. The flowers of both these species are shown in PLATE 33.

Our heaths and moorlands owe their great charm at this season largely to the heather and its near relations—the so-called bell heathers, or heaths. The commonest of these are the fine-leaved and the cross-leaved species—the latter at once recognisable not only by the cross-wise arrangement of its leaves, but also by its dense clusters of rosy, wax-like flowers.

Another favourite wild-flower of sunny heaths, and of dry places generally, is the graceful little harebell—the true bluebell of Scotland (PLATE 33). It should be noted that this plant is a campanula, and that it bears no relationship at all to the so-called bluebell of our spring woodlands, which is really a hyacinth.

PLATE 36.   JULY

SILVERWEED.

C. F. Newall.

THE HARD FERN.

Very different indeed from the flora of the dry heath is that of the inland water-side, whose vegetation is now, perhaps, more luxuriant than that of any other region in this country. Particularly impressive are the purple loosestrife, the great hairy willowherb, and the sweet-scented hemp agrimony—the centre of attraction for some of our handsomest butterflies.

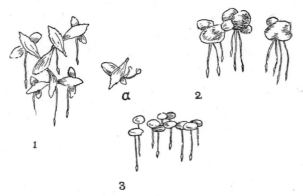

FIG. 20.—THREE COMMON DUCKWEEDS.

1. Ivy-leaved duckweed (*Lemna trisulca*).   2. Greater duckweed (*Lemna polyrrhiza*).
   (*a*) Frond bearing a flower.   3. Lesser duckweed (*Lemna minor*).

In the actual water itself the most striking plants are the two common waterlilies—the white and the yellow—but they are by no means alone. The Liliputian duckweeds and other of their interesting companions are illustrated in FIG. 20 and PLATE 24.

Among the more attractive wild-flowers of the July cornfields are the corn cockle and the cornflower. Both of them are almost certainly aliens, but they have been with us for so long, and are now so widely distributed, that they seem to belong to us. The corn cockle, unlike all its nearest relations in this country, is an annual plant, and is therefore encouraged rather than hindered by the plough.

A good many of our wild-flowers seem to have a special liking for waste places and waysides. The goutweed, the couchgrass, the henbane, the silverweed, the chicory, the ragwort and the cow parsnip are typical examples of such plants that can be found in flower during the present month. Illustrations of all of them are included in PLATES 31, 33, 34, 36, 43 and 46.

It is noteworthy that a considerable number of these plants of waste ground are of very wide distribution. There is not a single county in the British Isles, for example, where you cannot find the goutweed, the couchgrass, and the silverweed ; and even such less familiar plants as the tansy and the restharrow are missing from very few.

The henbane, on the other hand, in spite of its familiar name, is a comparative rarity. It may be common enough in some places, especially on sandy soils, but you may often search the countryside for scores of miles without finding a single specimen of it.

CHAPTER VIII

AUGUST

BIRD LIFE IN AUGUST

NO matter what the calendar may say to the contrary, August marks the opening of the autumn just as clearly as July marked the close of the summer. That is the case, at any rate, so far as our bird life is concerned.

It is true, of course, that summer sights and sounds are not entirely wanting. You may, for example, still see greenfinches, goldfinches, and yellowhammers feeding hungry broods of nestlings, and you may still hear the woodpigeon cooing as usual among the trees, or the corn bunting singing from the telegraph wires.

The fact remains, however, that the bulk of our bird observations during August will suggest autumn rather than summer. They will be concerned, that is, chiefly with such subjects as autumn song, autumn moulting, autumn migration and autumn flocks.

If you have listened carefully throughout the year to the songs —if such they can be called—of the great tit, the blue tit and the coal tit (PLATE 42), for example, you will have noticed that, with rare exceptions, they all ceased long before the end of July ; and we may look upon that cessation as marking the close of these birds' summer season.

Always, however, at some time during August—or at any rate

very early in September—these three tits begin to sing again.
Such August songs are in no sense a continuation of the songs of
summer, since, as we have just seen, those songs ended—almost
abruptly—in July. They are quite definitely an autumn event,
and will now continue, without another break, until the end of
the season.

A somewhat similar resumption of song is shown by the
starling (PLATE 42), for although there is no month in all the

FIG. 21.—TURNSTONES.

twelve when you cannot hear the song of this bird, it becomes
markedly less frequent in late June or early July. Then, after a
few weeks of almost complete silence, the starling sings again,
even more regularly than the tits.

These cessations and resumptions of song are, in the main,
closely connected with the birds' change of feathers, for August
is, above all else, the great moulting month. While the moult is
in progress, the birds often look most uncomfortable, and probably
feel so, too ; hence it is not altogether surprising that they have
little desire for song.

PLATE 38.   AUGUST

BLINDWORM AND FROGS.   109

HARVEST MOUSE.

LONG-TAILED FIELD MOUSE.

In July we noted the very first of the autumn migrants on their southward journey. They may, perhaps, have been a few pioneers only, but that will certainly not be the case during August. Many of our shore birds, for example—including the turnstones (FIG. 21)—are already moving in bulk, and even some inland species—notably the swift, the cuckoo and a few of the warblers—are quite definitely passing southwards.

Lastly, there are the beginnings of the great autumn flocks, with the endless problems which they present. For some time past, the lapwings and the starlings have shown this flocking tendency, but everywhere during August you will see that tendency grow ; and you must be careful not to mistake the newly formed flocks of our resident mistle-thrushes for newly arrived flocks of field-fares—those foreign thrushes which have scarcely yet begun to depart from their summer homes in northern Europe.

ANIMAL LIFE IN AUGUST

The warm days and nights of late summer afford ideal opportunities for watching the entertaining behaviour of most of our native mammals, both old and young.

The very attractive little harvest mouse (PLATE 39) could be seen much more frequently than it is, especially in southern and eastern England, if only it were sought in the right places. These include not merely fields of wheat and oats, but fields of beans too, and also, of course, the stacks that are made of these crops when they are gathered.

Gilbert White's description of this charming little animal and its globular nest—" so compact and well filled, that it would roll across the table without being discomposed, though it contained eight little mice that were naked and blind "—is always worth reading at this season.

The very varied nests of the long-tailed field mouse (PLATE 39) —which, as we noted last month, breeds all through the summer— are made not only in its burrows in the earth, but also often above ground. Sometimes you can find one of them in an old bird's nest, even when this is quite high in the hedgerow.

Animals which breed early in the year often have second, or even third, litters of young in late summer, and during this month and next you may expect to see new families, not only of rats and mice and rabbits, but also of hedgehogs, squirrels and dormice.

Reptiles and amphibians, both young and old, are prominent at this season too. Even when frogs leave the water, they prefer moist surroundings (PLATE 38), and it is interesting to notice their remarkable colour-changes in relation to their environment. Toads, on the other hand, are often found in relatively dry places.

The grass snake and the adder (PLATE 42) are both breeding during this month. Snakes' eggs are often found on manure heaps, sometimes in great masses, but the eggs of the adder hatch when they are laid, or even before.

Young fishes of all ages abound in suitable waters, for there has been continuous spawning since January. Of special interest at the present time are the later-breeding species, two of which— the tench and the minnow—are shown in PLATE 55.

Insect and other small life is abundant too, and eggs, larvae and pupae, as well as adults, can be found almost everywhere. Many butterflies and moths of second broods, or even of third, are now on the wing, including such familiar species as the wall, the

PLATE 40.   AUGUST

YOUNG WASPS EMERGING.

small heath, the small tortoiseshell, the common blue, the small copper and the small white.

The beautiful red underwing moth (PLATE 42) lays its eggs on poplars and willows, and must be sought in the vicinity of such trees, chiefly in southern and eastern England. The cranefly (shown in the same plate) is too abundant everywhere. Its emergence from the pupa, however, is one of those magical transformations that always hold the attention.

The number of wasps seems to grow daily at this season, but the annoyance which they cause is very small in proportion to the entertainment which they provide by their extraordinary instinctive behaviour. A glimpse of the emergence of the young is given in PLATE 40.

Wild life by the water-side is specially attractive just now. Though small in size, the whirligig beetles (FIG. 22) are certain to attract your attention by their mazy dances on the surface of the water. The larva of the whirligig (also shown in the figure) is a very remarkable little creature with two rows of abdominal gills behind its three pairs of legs.

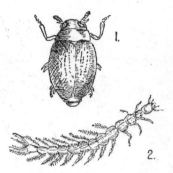

FIG. 22.—WHIRLIGIG AND ITS LARVA.

1. The adult beetle.
2. Larva, with abdominal gills.

PLANT LIFE IN AUGUST

The countryside in August is often even more parched than it was in July, and a good deal of our attention will therefore again

L

be devoted to those plants that are specially characteristic of moist and shady places.

There are relatively few plants that delay their first flowering until August, so that most of the blossoms that you find now will

Fig. 23.—THE FROGBIT.

not be new ones, but those of plants which have extended their flowering from earlier months.

The frogbit, the fleabane and the sundews, for instance, may all begin to flower in July, though it is often during August that they attract most attention. The frogbit is a plant of ponds and

---

KEY TO PLATE 42

1. Starling in song.	5. Coal tit.	9. Fleabane.
2. Red underwing moth.	6. Head of adder.	10. Cranefly.
3. Ripe fruits of birch.	7. Grass snake.	11. Broom fork-moss.
4. Ripe fruits of barberry.	8. Sundew.	12. Ink-cap fungi.

PLATE 42.   AUGUST

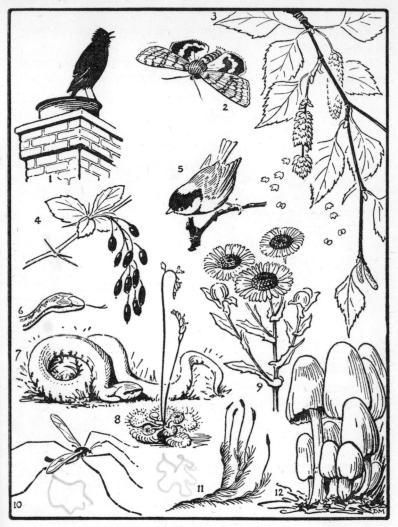

FROM AN AUGUST SKETCHBOOK.
(See opposite page.)

ditches; the fleabane, of marshes and damp roadsides; while the sundews are confined chiefly to bogs (FIG. 23 and PLATE 42).

A considerable number of flowerless plants, too, are characteristic of moist places in August, especially ferns, mosses and fungi. Two typical examples are the elegant little broom fork-moss and the very common ink-cap fungus, or inky toadstool, both of which are now conspicuous in shady woods (PLATE 42).

It is a fact worth remembering at this season that a good many plants acquire an altogether new interest as they pass from their flowering to their fruiting stages. Both flowers and fruits often need the help of wind and weather, as well as of insects and birds; and the multitudinous ways in which they secure such help are always worth investigating.

The common selfheal (PLATE 41) is a case in point, and if you will alternately dry and moisten its fruiting heads, you will have a practical demonstration of its quite unusual method of seed dispersal. Most plants tend to scatter their seeds in dry weather, but the selfheal, as you will find, reverses this procedure in a very interesting way.

A fair number of our trees and shrubs, too, including the birch and the barberry (PLATE 42), are becoming daily more interesting as their fruits mature. In that process, as well as in the beginning of autumn tints, you will see a clear indication that the summer season is at last drawing to a close.

CHAPTER IX

SEPTEMBER

BIRD LIFE IN SEPTEMBER

THE great autumn migrations, whose beginnings we noticed as far back as July, are now in full swing. Everywhere there are comings and goings. Sometimes the one preponderates and sometimes the other; and often you will see new arrivals from the north before the last of our summer visitors have departed for their winter homes in the south.

As we noted last month, some species leave us very early—puzzlingly early in the case of the swift and a few others. It is no uncommon thing to see swifts moving southwards even in July, and by the end of August most of them have usually gone. September swifts, in fact, are scarce enough in most places to be worth recording (PLATE 43).

And it is much the same with the cuckoos, for these birds also begin to leave us in July. Of special interest here, however, is the fact that it is always the *old* birds that go first. The cuckoos that you see in September, therefore, are generally *young* cuckoos. Exactly how they are able to follow in the wake of their neglectful parents is one of the secrets of the cuckoo that have not yet been cleared up.

Very often, of course, our summer visitors steal away silently and unobtrusively, but that is by no means always the case. Chiff-chaffs and willow warblers, for example, sing freely as they travel southwards, and you may often hear their farewell songs in quite unusual places at this season—just as you heard the calls of the wheatears when they passed northwards in spring.

Swallows and martins, too, may be seen flying southwards, often in conspicuous flocks. Hordes of foreign skylarks are arriving on our eastern seaboard from across the North Sea ; and

FIG. 24.—MAGPIE WITH GRUB.

from the Continent also, as well as from more northerly parts of our own country, come vast numbers of lapwings, accompanied, perhaps, by varying numbers of golden plover—at once distinguishable by their pointed wings, their rapid wing-strokes and their whistling calls.

In September, as in August, a good many birds resume their songs. The song-thrush and the skylark (PLATE 43), for example,

KEY TO PLATE 43

1. Ripe fruits of ash.	5. Chicory.	9. Mushrooms.
2. Swift.	6. Ragwort.	10. Common cord-moss.
3. Ivy in flower.	7. Skylark.	11. Harvest-spider, or harvestman.
4. Garden spider in web.	8. Giant wood-wasp.	12. Herald moth.

PLATE 43.   SEPTEMBER

FROM A SEPTEMBER SKETCHBOOK.
(*See opposite page.*)

often sing freely towards the end of the month, and even the black-bird may occasionally be heard.   Among the ripening thistle-heads you may hear the silvery notes of goldfinches (*Frontispiece*), while starlings and robins are singing almost as regularly as in spring.

The farmer's autumn ploughings afford many opportunities for observing the feeding habits of some of our larger birds. The much-maligned magpie (FIG. 24), for example, does great service at this season in its wholesale destruction of insects, larvae, pupae, millipedes, slugs, snails and field-mice.

ANIMAL LIFE IN SEPTEMBER

So far as our native mammals are concerned, September is largely a month of transition from summer to autumn, and many little signs of the coming season will become evident as the month wears away.

The coat of the young fox, for instance, will be losing its greyish tint and becoming more yellow ; the squirrel will begin to collect and to bury some of the great harvest of food that is now available ; and on many a path and trackway you will see the dead bodies of shrews—bodies that show no sign whatever of disease or accident.

This autumn death of the shrews has attracted the attention of country dwellers for generations.   In some parts the old belief that a shrew cannot cross a human pathway without "dropping down dead" is still current; and even to-day it is difficult to give a wholly adequate explanation of this strangely high autumn mortality.

In September the spider season is at its best, and there is no end

---

KEY TO PLATE 44

1. Water Boatman.	3. Larva of Great Water Beetle.	5. Brown Water Beetle (female).
2. Great Water Beetle.	4. Brown Water Beetle (male).	6. Larva of Brown Water Beetle.
	7. Water Scorpion.	

PLATE 44.   SEPTEMBER

POND INSECTS.
(*See opposite page.*)

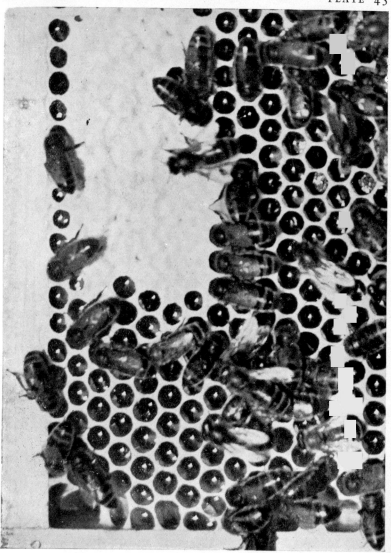

to the interest that these abundant little animals can afford, even to a casual observer of their ways. The so-called harvest-spiders (PLATE 43), which are so conspicuous everywhere just now, can be distinguished from the true spiders (PLATE 43 and FIG. 25) by the complete absence of a waist.

Butterflies and moths are still plentiful, though a good many species have now disappeared, and others are becoming scarcer. Some, too, are already going into hibernation. Thus the small tortoiseshell does not always wait until October before retiring (FIG. 28) ; nor does the herald moth (PLATE 43), whose awakening we noted in April.

The so-called giant wood-wasp (PLATE 43), in spite of her yellow-and-black colour, her humming flight

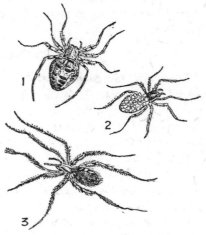

FIG. 25.—THREE COMMON SPIDERS.

1. Garden spider (*Epeira diademata*).
2. Wolf spider (*Lycosa*) with young spiderlings on her back.
3. House spider (*Tegenaria domestica*).

and her sting-like "tail," is not really a wasp at all, and is quite harmless—at any rate to human beings. The apparent sting is used for boring holes in trees, in which her eggs are laid.

All through the summer and autumn the insect life of ponds and streams is of particular interest, affording, as it does, not only many glimpses of finely specialised adaptations to a watery

M

environment, but also many episodes in some of the most fascinating of all life histories. Some typical specimens are shown in PLATE 44.

And the life of the hive bee is similarly crowded with interesting events, from the emergence of the first workers in early spring to that appalling massacre of the drones which takes place at the approach of winter. A peep at the work inside the hive is given in PLATE 45.

PLANT LIFE IN SEPTEMBER

September, like August, has very few wild-flowers that can truly be called its own. It is largely a month of lingering blossoms and ripening fruits, though it need not, of course, be any the less interesting because of that. It provides, in fact, a great wealth of botanical material for study and investigation.

In a good many parts of the country just now, for instance, you can find the flowers of two quite different plants, both of which are known as autumn crocuses. One of them (*Crocus nudiflorus*) is a *true* crocus, but the other, in spite of its crocus-like appearance, is not a crocus at all. Its proper name is meadow saffron (*Colchicum autumnale*).

It has often been said that the meadow saffron is the plant from which the saffron of commerce is obtained, but that is a mistake. Saffron comes from an autumn crocus (*Crocus sativus*) which is a *true* crocus, but which is quite different from the true crocus mentioned above, and which is not likely to be found anywhere in this country away from cultivation.

Towards the end of the month you may watch the flowering of the ivy (PLATE 43), and you may watch also the last stages of ripening in the fruits of the sycamore (FIG. 26), the maple, the ash

PLATE 46.   SEPTEMBER

THE COW PARSNIP.

PLATE 47

THE CORN SOWTHISTLE.

(PLATE 43), the horse chestnut and a number of other trees, to say nothing of almost innumerable plants.

In PLATES 43, 46 and 47 are shown a few of September's lingering blossoms, some of which have already been referred to in earlier notes ; but it would be easy to extend the list indefinitely.

In the September stubbles alone, for instance, you may find the flowers of several kinds of speedwells, toadflaxes, camomiles, cudweeds, fumitories, tares, deadnettles, hempnettles, docks, thistles and goosefoots, while such attractive little plants as the wild pansy

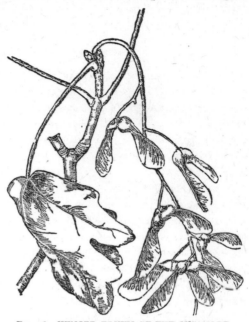

FIG. 26.—WINGED FRUITS OF THE SYCAMORE.

and the scarlet pimpernel will be flowering there all through the month.

Many of our flowerless plants, too, are now becoming prominent, especially the fungi and the mosses. A typical example of each of these great groups is shown in PLATE 43.

CHAPTER X

OCTOBER

BIRD LIFE IN OCTOBER

OCTOBER, like September, is largely a month of bird movements, the chief difference being that the arrivals will now attract more attention than the departures. Regular and irregular visitors of the most varied kinds are flocking almost daily to this country from colder lands to the north and the east, and even our own resident birds may be changing their quarters in surprisingly large numbers.

Among the most familiar of the October new-comers are the redwing and the fieldfare—two foreign thrushes from Scandinavia and other parts of northern Europe (PLATE 48). It must be remembered, however, that although we usually speak of these birds as autumn migrants, they occasionally arrive in small numbers as early as August, or even July.

It is not usually until October, however, that they become widely and generally distributed. A very familiar sound of October nights is the thin, penetrating flight-call of the redwings ; and in the fields by day you see flocks of fieldfares everywhere,

---

KEY TO PLATE 48

1. Ripening beech nuts.	5. Yarrow.	9. House spider.
2. Ripening sweet chestnuts.	6. Corn marigold.	10. Cypress feather-moss.
3. Winter moths, female and male.	7. Redwing.	11. Pixie-cup lichen.
4. Fieldfare.	8. Death's-head moth.	12. Footprints of house mouse.

PLATE 48.

OCTOBER

FROM AN OCTOBER SKETCHBOOK.
(*See opposite page.*)

and hear their harsh calls—sounding like *cha-cha-cha-chak*—as they pass overhead.

In January we noted the bramblings feeding with chaffinches under the beech trees, but it is in October that the main arrivals of these foreign finches take place. They stay in Britain throughout the winter, and leave us chiefly during March, April and May. A brambling that was ringed in Cheshire in February was found in Yugo-Slavia in the following July.

FIG. 27.—GREAT GREY SHRIKE.

During October, too, our own native bird populations are often greatly augmented by visitors from abroad. Rooks, crows and jackdaws, for instance, arrive in vast numbers on various parts of the east coast, and so also do greenfinches, tree sparrows, yellowhammers and many other familiar species.

And among lesser-known October arrivals, special watch should

PLATE 49.

OCTOBER

WATER VOLES.

THE EDIBLE FROG.

be kept for such interesting visitors as hooded crows, siskins, redpolls, snow buntings and great grey shrikes. These last-named are larger birds than our own red-backed shrikes, and may be seen perched like sentinels in conspicuous places (FIG. 27).

October is a rather poor month for bird song. The most regular singers are probably the starling, the robin and the dipper, though in favourable circumstances you may often hear the wren, the hedge-sparrow, the skylark, the goldcrest, the linnet, the goldfinch, the corn bunting and the woodpigeon, and even the song-thrush, the mistle-thrush and a few late chiffchaffs.

ANIMAL LIFE IN OCTOBER

In early October there is still much activity in the animal world, even among those species that spend the winter in a state of hibernation. The dormouse, for instance, is still foraging for food, and so also are snakes, lizards, frogs, toads and newts. Towards the end of the month, however, all these winter sleepers will vanish from our sight.

The edible frog (PLATE 50) is unknown in most parts of this country, but may be found in a few Midland and East Anglian counties. It is rather larger than the common frog, and seldom strays far from its native pond or stream.

Very typical activities of the month are the collection and storage of winter food supplies. The squirrel (PLATE 51) is perhaps the most conspicuous food-storer, but by no means the only one. The long-tailed field mouse is a tireless hoarder of trifles, and even the water voles (PLATE 49) will sometimes lay by a reserve of succulent roots and stems.

The house mouse, too, is a confirmed collector of viands, not merely in autumn, but the whole year through. It wanders a good deal at changes of the seasons, and its tell-tale footprints (PLATE 48) can often be found in the most unexpected places.

October is almost as good a month as September for the study of spiders, and of their often peculiar distribution. The common house spider (PLATE 48), for instance, is only very rarely found out of doors, whereas one of its very near relations never enters the house.

FIG. 28.—SMALL TORTOISESHELL BUTTERFLY.

The insect is hibernating in a ceiling corner.

Butterfly life wanes markedly as the days grow colder. Small whites, small coppers, common blues, commas and a number of others are still on the wing, but red admirals, peacocks and the last of the small tortoiseshells (FIG. 28) are now all seeking quarters for the winter.

On potato haulms in September and October you may sometimes find the giant caterpillar of the death's-head moth; and the giant moth itself (PLATE 48) may still be on the wing. Some interesting new-comers of the month are the winter moths, whose females are totally incapable of flight (PLATE 48).

PLANT LIFE IN OCTOBER

So far as our wild-flowers are concerned, October must be looked upon as a month of retreat. Yet although the blossoms

136

THE SQUIRREL IN AUTUMN.   137

Photos: Richard Morse, F.L.S.

BROKEN SHELLS.

Above : Stone used by thrush for the breaking of snails' shells.
Below : Hazel-nut shells wedged in tree-trunk by nuthatch.

of late summer and early autumn are fast disappearing from the countryside, a good many still hold on, and it is pleasant to notice how very persistent some of these are—the yarrow and the corn marigold, for example (PLATE 48).

The daily diminishing number of flowers, however, brings at least one compensating advantage, for it allows a greater amount of time to be devoted to the more accurate identification of those that can still be found—the puzzling speedwells, mayweeds and camomiles, for example, and the still more puzzling fumitories, docks and goosefoots.

Wild fruits, too, are of special interest in October, not only in themselves, but because of their great value as an aid to identification. They include not only those of many trees and shrubs, among which the beech and the sweet chestnut stand out conspicuously (PLATE 48), but also those of a large number of flowering plants.

Then there are the autumn tints of the leaves. Ever since August this tinting has been going on, and now at last it has reached the pinnacle of its beauty. The month of October, indeed, provides a feast of colour in our woodlands and hedgerows which can scarcely be outdone by any other month in the year. It is a feast, moreover, which the scientist, as well as the artist, can greatly enjoy.

And always, as the wild-flowers retreat at the approach of winter, our flowerless plants come more strongly into evidence. The fungi, for instance, are now at their best, and everywhere you can find mosses and lichens of unending variety in the very heydey of their lives (PLATE 48).

N

CHAPTER XI

NOVEMBER

Bird Life in November

THE bird life of November is not, as a rule, strikingly different from that of October. Its outstanding feature, perhaps, is the migratory movements of many species, though such movements naturally become less and less conspicuous as autumn passes gradually into winter.

FIG. 29.—THE BLUE TIT.

As was the case last month, our interest will lie chiefly in arrivals, for winter visitors will continue to reach us throughout the month. Nevertheless, many of our familiar summer migrants are still with us, and on any day you may see a belated swallow or martin passing overhead, or even catch a glimpse of a still more belated swift or young cuckoo.

Interesting movements, too, can still be observed among our resident birds, many of which continue to leave us in considerable numbers. We know that some of our native skylarks, for instance, cross to France at this season, while others, flying westwards, take up their winter quarters in Ireland.

Even our familiar blackbirds and thrushes are far from being sedentary birds. It is true that many of our song-thrushes are singing regularly at this season (PLATE 53), but it is true also that many of them, as ringing experiments have shown, are passing westwards to Ireland, or southwards to France, Spain and Portugal.

Many of the tits, too, are becoming obviously uneasy about the approach of winter, and are daily drawing nearer and nearer to

FIG. 30.—COMMON BUZZARD, SOARING.

our houses, in the hope of thus securing more regular and more generous supplies of food (FIG. 29).

Among the more conspicuous of the November immigrants are the woodpigeons (PLATE 53), which, in some years, arrive in vast numbers on our eastern seaboard, and spread gradually westwards. Very often these hordes of hungry new-comers do immense harm in the fields, utterly ruining many of the farmers' winter crops.

But apart altogether from the larger aspects of November bird

141

life, many interesting observations can be made in almost any part of the country. The majestic buzzard, for instance, is often on the move at this season, and may suddenly appear in the most unexpected quarters (FIG. 30).

Along many a hedge-bank, too, you can find the stone on which the song-thrush has hammered the few remaining snails that he can find (PLATE 52) ; and on many a tree-bole you can see where the nuthatch has, in his own clever way, hacked to pieces the hard shells of the hazel-nuts for the sake of the precious kernels within (PLATE 52).

ANIMAL LIFE IN NOVEMBER

With the coming of November, life in the animal world undergoes a marked change. One after another the hibernating species disappear, while the hunting species—the weasels, the stoats and the foxes—often become increasingly fierce, bold and cunning with the growing scarcity of food.

Even so untamable a creature as the wild cat (PLATE 54) will draw nearer to farms and homesteads when it feels the pangs of hunger. We must be careful, however, to distinguish between this now rare animal and the comparatively common half-wild cats, which are merely escapes from domestication—or the descendants of such.

If a close watch be kept upon our native mammals from November onwards, it will be found that it is impossible to draw

---

KEY TO PLATE 53

1. November moth.	5. Devil's-bit scabious.	9. Rat.
2. Woodpigeon.	6. Chestnut moth.	10. Wavy hair-moss.
3. Plane twig, with fruits.	7. Hoary lichen (*Evernia prunastri*).	11. Snails hibernating.
4. Twig of false acacia.	8. Song-thrush.	12. Creeping buttercup.

PLATE 53.   NOVEMREB

FROM A NOVEMBER SKETCHBOOK.
(*See opposite page.*)

a hard and fast line between those which retire in winter and those which do not. The dormouse always retires ; the rat (PLATE 53) probably never. Between those two extremes, however, are the voles, which lie low in severe weather, but which are very active when it is mild (PLATE 54).

Among fishes, too, a number of interesting responses to seasonal changes can be seen. The carp, for example, retires to deeper waters at the onset of winter—often in groups of fifty or more individuals—while the tench (PLATE 55) even buries itself in the mud, and remains torpid until the spring.

But perhaps the soundest of all winter sleepers are the snails, which, like the carp and many other hibernators, are fond of company in their retirement (PLATE 53). Normally they awaken in the spring, but occasionally they oversleep until another spring, and appear to be none the worse for their long fast.

Butterfly life, at any rate so far as the activities of the perfect insect are concerned, is now practically at an end, though an unusually warm day may tempt a few of the hibernating species —such as the peacock and the small tortoiseshell—from their hiding-places.

The moths of the month, on the other hand, form a quite considerable list, some being survivors from earlier months, and others new-comers. Among these latter may be the appropriately named November and chestnut moths, both of which are shown in PLATE 53.

PLANT LIFE IN NOVEMBER

During November the wild-flowers of summer and autumn continue to retreat before the oncoming winter. The great majority of them, in fact, are steadily vanishing from sight, and the present month affords, therefore, an excellent opportunity for inquiring into the various ways in which the different species are able, as it were, to outwit the cold season.

In the case of a typical annual plant—the corn poppy, for example—the plant itself, as an individual, perishes utterly, leaving only its extremely hardy seeds to survive the winter. Perennial plants, on the other hand, survive *as individuals*, retiring into their underground organs until the winter is over.

The actual date when a plant ceases to flower, however, depends very largely upon the weather, and unless this is unusually severe you should still be able to gather an interesting bouquet of wild-flowers on almost any country walk. The white campion, the red clover, the wild pansy, the yarrow and the corn marigold, for example, often flower freely in November, and so also do the creeping buttercup and the devil's-bit scabious (PLATE 53).

Most of our trees and shrubs, like the perennial plants already mentioned, retire for the winter, but instead of retiring into the earth, they withdraw, as it were, into their own woody tissues, throwing off the whole of their summer foliage in the process.

The naked twigs of the trees, two examples of which are shown in PLATE 53, are objects of much interest to the field botanist, not only in themselves, but also because of the very varied lichen flora which they—as well as the trunks—so frequently bear (PLATE 53).

Fungi and mosses, too, are abundant everywhere in November. The beautiful wavy hair-moss (PLATE 53) grows in woods and other moist places, and is at its best during autumn and winter.

CHAPTER XII

DECEMBER

Bird Life in December

THE makers of our calendar have decided that the major part of December shall belong to the season of autumn, and the naturalist fully agrees with this decision, for it is usually very easy to find unmistakable signs of that season in all parts of the countryside.

Fig. 31.—PTARMIGAN IN THE SNOW.

The robin (PLATE 58), for instance, whose autumn song became noticeable as far back as August, is singing just as freely to-day as he was then, and much the same can be said also of such birds as the song-thrush and the dipper.

Many other birds, too, if weather conditions are reasonably

PLATE 54.   NOVEMBER

Above: WILD CAT.   *Below:* VOLE EATING APPLE.

Above : MINNOWS. *Below :* COMMON TENCH.

favourable, will sing more or less regularly, or at any rate intermittently, throughout the month. The wren (PLATE 58) is a conspicuous example of such singers, and so also is the hedgesparrow, the corn bunting or the woodpigeon.

Moreover, although autumn migration has now slowed down to a very low ebb, it has not entirely ceased. Stragglers of many kinds, including both swallows and martins, are often recorded in December, especially in coastal districts, and some have been known to stay with us until Christmas, or even later than that.

There is such a season, of course, as a British winter, as the snow-white ptarmigan (FIG. 31) may serve to remind us, but for the naturalist, at any rate, there is certainly no such thing as a " dead " season at any time of the year.

It is true that there may, even in southern Britain, be severe spells of cold during the darker months—spells which often take a heavy toll of bird life—but the fact remains that you can always see signs of autumn in the dullest of Decembers, and always signs of spring when once a new year has begun.

ANIMAL LIFE IN DECEMBER

In very severe weather animal life in general may, of course, reach a low ebb, but in all ordinary circumstances even the dullest of Decembers will show abundant signs of activity. It is, indeed, surprising to find how many of our native mammals can be seen abroad during the month, if only careful watch be kept in the right places.

Such species as foxes, weasels and stoats (PLATE 57) are, of course, always active. Badgers and hedgehogs may occasionally

o

be seen, and squirrels are still quite common (PLATE 57), while rats and rabbits, even in December, may be producing young. The footprints of most of these animals, and of several others besides, form an interesting study on winter walks (PLATE 58).

The stoat among mammals, like the ptarmigan among birds (FIG. 31), is famous for its white winter coat, which makes it almost invisible on the snow-covered ground. In southern Britain, however, white stoats are rare. In the Highlands of Scotland they can be seen everywhere.

We saw last month that our native species of voles usually become more or less torpid in severe weather, and the same is true of the long-tailed field mouse. The shrews, on the other hand, appear to be active at all times, and so also do the moles, though they certainly tunnel more deeply when the temperature is low.

The only butterflies of December are occasional hibernated specimens. Moths, on the other hand, are relatively common, and a typical new-comer of the month is shown in PLATE 58.

Everywhere, too, you can find signs of the *activities* of insects, even if the insects themselves are not in evidence. The strange little burrowings of the bark beetles, for instance, are specially worthy of a close investigation (PLATE 58).

PLANT LIFE IN DECEMBER

Last month we noticed how a typical annual plant perished at the onset of winter, surviving only in its seeds until the coming of another spring. Very common in December, however, are a

PLATE 56   DECEMBER

Richard Morse, F.L.S.

THE OAK IN WINTER.

Above: THE RED SQUIRREL. *Below:* THE STOAT.

number of so-called annuals which often survive the winter *as individuals.*

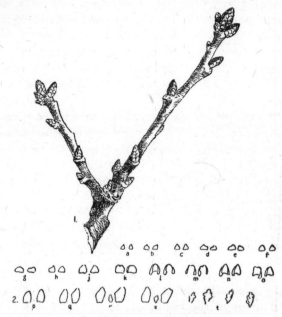

FIG. 32.—OAK TWIG IN DECEMBER.

1. Twig with winter buds.
2. Bud dissected, showing relation of scales to foliage leaves.
  a-q. First sixteen pairs of scales, showing no trace of leaves.
  r, s. Scales subtending leaves.
  t. Young foliage leaves.

The chickweed, the shepherd's purse and the groundsel are typical examples of such plants. They have no real resting season at all, but in favourable circumstances are able to produce a continuous succession of generations all the year round (PLATE 58, and also PLATE 3).

Very typical of December wild-flowers, too, are stragglers from earlier months. The number of these will vary a good deal from year to year, but in mild seasons you will have little difficulty in finding the lingering blossoms of such plants as charlock, wild radish, thyme-leaved sandwort, field lady's mantle and yarrow, together with buttercups, dandelions and speedwells in plenty.

Now that our deciduous trees have lost their summer foliage, their characteristic forms stand out very clearly across the landscape, giving to each species an individuality that is usually recognisable at a glance (PLATE 56). It is, nevertheless, often interesting to substantiate one's diagnosis by a closer study of the bare twigs (FIG. 32, and also FIGS. 2, 4, 7 and 10).

Probably the most familiar wild fruits of December are those of the holly and the mistletoe (PLATE 58) but a number of others can always be found, including those of the ivy, which are still hard and green.

Flowerless plants continue to flourish everywhere. The quaint little candle-snuff fungus gives a living interest to many an old stump; and the tamarisk feather-moss, now in fruit, is one of the loveliest of all our woodland mosses (PLATE 58).

KEY TO PLATE 58

1. December moth.	5. Wren.	9. Trail of rat, walking.
2. Robin.	6. Burrows of bark-beetle.	10. Tamarisk feather-moss.
3. Mistletoe.	7. Common chickweed.	11. Candle-snuff fungus.
4. Holly.	8. Shepherd's purse.	12. Trail of rat, jumping.

PLATE 58.

DECEMBER

FROM A DECEMBER SKETCHBOOK.
(*See opposite page.*)

INDEX

INDEX

PRINTED IN GREAT BRITAIN BY
MORRISON AND GIBB LTD., LONDON AND EDINBURGH